PROGRAM DESIGN IN PHYSICAL EDUCATION

A GUIDE TO THE DEVELOPMENT OF EXEMPLARY PROGRAMS

PAUL VOGEL, Ph.D.
VERN SEEFELDT, Ph.D

Michigan State University

Benchmark Press, Inc.
Indianapolis, Indiana

Copyright © 1988, by Benchmark Press, Inc.

ALL RIGHTS RESERVED.

Reproduction or translation of any part of this work beyond that permitted by Sections 107 and 108 United States Copyright Act without the permission of the copyright owner is unlawful. Requests for permission should be addressed to Publisher, Benchmark Press, Inc., 8435 Keystone Crossing, Suite 175, Indianapolis, IN 46240.

Library of Congress Cataloging in Publication Data:

VOGEL, PAUL 1939-

PROGRAM DESIGN IN PHYSICAL EDUCATION:
A GUIDE TO THE DEVELOPMENT OF EXEMPLARY PROGRAMS

Cover Design: Gary Schmitt
Copy Editor: Kendal Gladish

Library of Congress Catalog Card number: 88-070144

ISBN: 0936157-29-1

Printed in the United States of America
10 9 8 7 6 5 4 3 2 1

The Publisher and Author disclaim responsibility for any adverse effects or consequences from the misapplication or injudicious use of the information contained within this text.

Table of Contents

Acknowledgments

Preface

Chapter 1: Need for Exemplary Physical Education Programs
    Need for Change 1
    Definition of an Exemplary Program 2

Chapter 2: Program Design: An Overview of the Outcomes and Procedures
    Outcomes of Program Improvement 3
    Overview of the Curriculum design Model 4
    Overview of the Steps Involved in Program Improvement . . .7

Chapter 3: Contributions of Physical Activity to Well-Being
    Categories of Outcomes associated with Physical Activity . . .9

Chapter 4: Development of Relevant and Defensible Goals
    Rationale for Community Involvement 13
    Assigning Importance to the Contributions 14
    Stating Appropriate Program Goals 15

Chapter 5: Development of Program and Instructional Objectives
    Identifying Program Objectives 19
    Identification of Instructional Objectives 20

Chapter 6: Organization of the K-12 Curriculum
    Procedures for Developing a Curriculum structure 25

Chapter 7: Designing Effective Instruction
    Design of Effective Instruction 35
    Guidelines for Effective Instruction 38

Chapter 8: Developing Resource Materials
    The Need for Resource Materials 45
    Instructional Resource Materials 47
    Summary 49

Chapter 9: Evaluation of Student Status and Progress
    Key Features of Student Evaluation 63
    Summary 71

Chapter 10: Program Evaluation
    Program Evaluation Defined 73
    Purpose of Program Evaluation 74
    Evaluation for Program Improvement 74
    Evaluation for Program Effectiveness 75
    Summary 81

References

Appendix A
    Criteria for Program Evaluation

Appendix B
    Guidelines for Effective Educational Change

Appendix C
    Materials for Conducting a Self-study

Appendix D
    Contributions of Physical Activity to Well-Being

Appendix E
    Reported Outcomes Obtained Through Participation in Physical Education Programs

Appendix F
    Rating the Importance of Potential Contributions of Physical Activity and Physical Education to Well-Being

Appendix G
    Examples of Goals and Program Objectives for Physical Education

Appendix H
    Selection, Placement, and Estimation of Needed Instructional Time for Program Objectives

Appendix I
    Example Instructional Materials and Forms

Appendix J
    Student Performance Score Sheet

Acknowledgments

The ideas expressed in this book represent the contributions of many individuals—former teachers, students, and colleagues. We find it impossible to recognize all of them or even to recall their names. Many of them made their contributions unknowingly through questions that challenged us to review our positions and restate our ideas. Much of the information has been distilled and revised many times, beginning with the Battle Creek Physical Education Curriculum Project in the middle and late 1960's, continuing with the I CAN Project of the 1970's and, more recently, in the East Lansing Physical Education Curriculum Project and the Michigan Exemplary Physical Education Programs Project, the latter a five-year project in curriculum revision sponsored by the Michigan Association for Health, Physical Education, Recreation, and Dance. Although each of these ventures has added immeasurably to the views reflected in this book, we would like to dedicate this effort to the staff of the East Lansing Public Schools, for it was through their faith, confidence, and perseverance that this process was permitted to unfold when it frequently would have been easier to succumb to the pressures of returning to older, more comfortable ways of providing physical education programs for students.

We are especially indebted to the following individuals.

Work Committee Members

Chip Frentz and Dona Rae Vogel (elementary schools)
Nick Archer, Linda Nelson, and Kay Stanek (middle schools)
Jack Bamford, Kitty Mitchell, and Jack Piotter (high school)

Curriculum Coordinators

Gary Davis, John Fitzpatrick, and Jerry Kusler

Superintendents

Robert Docking and William Mitchell

We are also indebted to School Board Members who consistently supported efforts to obtain exemplary programs in all phases of the project and at all levels of the East Lansing Public School Curriculum. Their dedication during the development, implementation, and evaluation of these materials is deeply appreciated.

Paul Vogel
Vern Seefeldt

Preface

A primary purpose of this book is to provide a means for shifting the emphasis in K-12 physical education programs from "instructional inputs or activities" to "student outcomes." Physical educators have an excellent opportunity to ensure that students obtain numerous benefits through their participation in a K-12 program. The contributions of physical activity to well-being have been well documented and provide an excellent base from which to design or redesign physical education programs. Many individuals, including parents, administrators, and fellow educators (those who control the resources for our programs) do not believe, however that participation in physical education produces these valued benefits. It is important, therefore, for physical educators to clearly describe the outcomes of their programs and educate their constituent groups regarding the importance of physical education to well-being and performance. Even more important is the need to implement sound programs and evaluate the degree to which students achieve the intended benefits. Until proponents of physical education programs can produce evidence that they can effectively use limited resources, they are unlikely to receive the resources necessary to obtain the outcomes that could result from comprehensive K-12 programs.

This book provides a set of procedures and forms that promote systematic planning, implementation, and evaluation of K-12 programs of physical education. The forms and procedures were developed for use in school districts, but they are also appropriate for inclusion in pre-service education programs. The focus of the chapters is on structuring the curriculum and organizing instruction in a way that provides defensible answers to the following questions:

- "What content should be included in the K-12 physical education program?" and, perhaps more importantly, "Why would this content be included?"
- When should the selected content be taught within and across grade levels?
- How should instruction be implemented to provide the best opportunity to maximize students' achievements?
- What are the effects of the program on students' performance?
- What improvements can be made in the program to increase its effectiveness or efficiency?

The chapters and appendices of this book are written to help physical educators plan, implement, and evaluate programs in a way that facilitates obtaining evidence of effectiveness. This evaluation-based approach to program improvement will suggest what revisions should be made whenever the criteria for establishing evidence of effectiveness have not been met.

Paul Vogel
Vern Seefeldt

Chapter 1

Need for Exemplary Physical Education Programs

Physical activity, as an important component in modern day lifestyles, currently has more acceptance by the public in general than at any other time in recent history. Also, physical educators have more evidence regarding the beneficial effects of activity on well-being. Public acceptance of physical activity and knowledge of its influence on well-being, in combination with the recent research on effective teaching and schooling, consititute the necessary ingredients for physical educators to provide outstanding programs for school-age children.

Although all of the necessary ingredients for excellence are at our disposal, programs of physical education are experiencing more erosion of resources (time, staff, equipment, facilities, materials) than at any other time in the history of our profession. Although there is no single cause or reason to explain this paradox, it appears that the lack of administrative and public support for physical education is based upon the belief that participation in physical education programs does not cause students to achieve the program's anticipated benefits. Even if this perception is incorrect, it restricts the resources allocated to implement physical education programs.

NEED FOR CHANGE

Public support for physical education will continue to erode unless there are significant alterations in the outcomes of many of the nation's programs. There is currently little agreement among members of the profession regarding what content should be included in the curriculum. Without clear specification of content (preferably in terms of valued student outcomes) it is difficult, if not impossible, to select effective instructional approaches or to determine whether or not a program is efficient or effective. The time is long overdue for professional physical educators to:

1. specify program intent in terms of clearly stated program goals and objectives;
2. select and implement instructional activities and methods that facilitate the attainment of stated objectives;
3. evaluate the degree to which the desired outcomes are obtained; and

4. alter program content and/or methodology as needed so that students' achievements of stated objectives are realized.

The inclination of physical education teachers to blame low levels of support on a lack of equipment, limited facilities, large class sizes, and/or crowded teaching schedules has not motivated school boards and administrators to restore resources to physical education programs. Strategically, a more fruitful approach for restoration of resources appears to involve a systematic inspection of what we are teaching, why it is being taught, where the content is emphasized in the K-12 program, how instruction is delivered, and whether or not an appropriate number of high-priority objectives can be achieved. Evidence demonstrating that a limited number of high-priority objectives can be achieved with existing resources provides a strong base from which to request the resources necessary to achieve important but lower priority objectives.

DEFINITION OF AN EXEMPLARY PROGRAM

Exemplary physical education programs, as the term is used in this book, must meet three broad criteria. First, the intended outcomes of the program must be appropriate (defensible and relevant). Second, the program's implementation procedures must be described sufficiently well so that they can be replicated. Third, there must be evidence of significant student achievement in the intended outcomes of the program. An overview of the characteristics of an exemplary program is included in Chapter 2. The other chapters of the book provide materials and procedures that can be used to design or redesign programs in a way that facilitates their potential to meet the criteria for classification as an exemplary physical education program.

Chapter 2

Program Design: An Overview of the Outcomes and Procedures

The contents of this book provide an approach to program improvement that is designed to result in exemplary programs. This chapter briefly describes the outcome of implementing a set of procedures designed to improve programs, overviews the curriculum design process, and explains steps that can be taken to obtain the desired program characteristics.

OUTCOMES OF PROGRAM IMPROVEMENT

Appropriate implementation of the steps outlined in subsequent chapters is designed to result in the outcomes listed in Figure 2-1.

1. A defensible statement of goals which is representative of and supportable by the community.

2. A list of program objectives that have been selected to operationalize each goal statement.

3. A K-12 organizational structure which identifies the order within which the program objectives are taught across grade levels.

4. Designation of the objectives that should be included (and excluded) in the program in accordance with changing district resources.

5. Identification of the performance criteria that define instructional levels within each program objective.

6. An implementation model (based upon the current research on effective instruction) that will guide the design of instructional interventions.

7. A statement describing procedures for guiding the district's student evaluation model.

8. A statement describing procedures for guiding the evaluation and revision of the curriculum and instructional model.

Figure 2.1. Program improvement outcomes

The outcomes briefly described above are expressed in more specific terms as criteria for program evaluation in Appendix A. In this appendix characteristics of an exemplary program are followed by a brief statement written to further explain the meaning of the criterion statement. Figure 2-2 illustrates two of the 10 criteria included in this Appendix. Application of the steps described in Chapters 3 through 10 is intended to result in programs that meet each of these criteria.

CRITERIA FOR PROGRAM EVALUATION

1. Program Purpose: The intended outcomes of the physical education program are stated as goals that represent documented evidence of the relationship between physical activity and health and performance.

   Interpretation:

   Program goals must represent more than broad, general statements of instructional intent. They must express a belief about what can and should be the purpose of a physical education program, and clearly be related to the evidence that enumerates the contributions of activity to human well-being. Goal statements are written as outcomes (i.e., they represent the results of instruction, rather than instructional processes or opportunities).

2. Relevant Goals: Goals are proposed by professional educators, through consultation with community representatives, to ensure relevance of content to local situations.

   Interpretation:

   This criterion measures the degree to which the content of the program, as stated in the goals, represents outcomes that are viewed as important and relevant by representatives of the local community. Such information should be obtained from administrators, teachers, parents, students, school board members, and others. It should then be used to finalize the goals and/or the relative emphasis the goals are to receive while implementing the physical education program.

Figure 2.2. Example of the program evaluation criteria included in Appendix A

OVERVIEW OF THE CURRICULUM DESIGN MODEL

Figure 2-3 provides a schematic illustration of the process involved in the development or redesign of programs of physical education. The model uses two primary sources of information: the documented contributions of physical activity to well-being, and information related to effective organization and implementation of educational programs. The contributions of activity to well-being provide the base for program content (goals and objectives), and the information related to effective organization (*i.e.*, principles of effective instruction and schooling, growth and developmental characteristics of students, and the process of educational change[1]) provides the base of information necessary to systematically organize, implement, and evaluate the program.

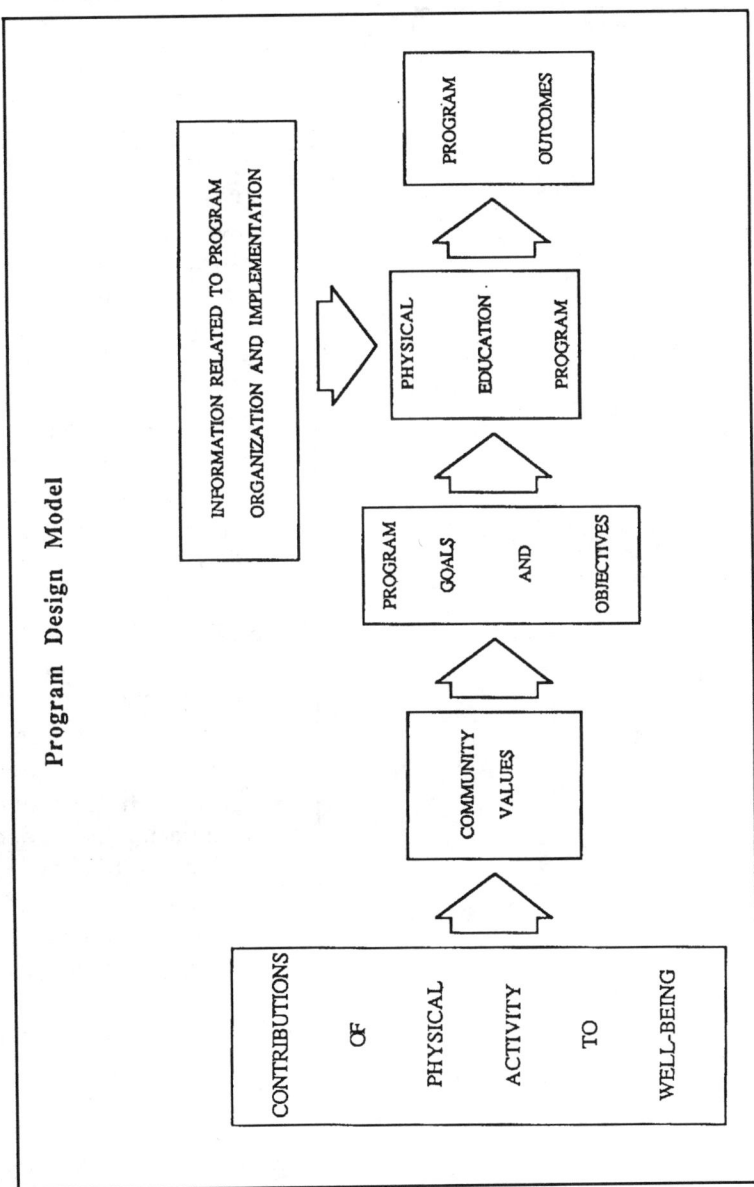

Figure 2.3. A model for the design of physical education programs

As illustrated in Figure 2-3, the potential outcomes of physical education have their source in the documented contributions of activity to well-being. These contributions are presented and rated for their relative importance by selected members of the

1. See Appendix B, "*Guidelines for Instituting Effective Educational Change.*"

local community and subsequently converted into statements of goals and program objectives. This process produces relevant and defensible statements of program intent. Using information drawn from the literature on children, effective instruction,

---

Suggested Sequence of Events that Lead to the Development of an Exemplary Physical Education Program

1. Define and document the contributions of physical activity to physical and mental health.
2. Represent these contributions as potential outcomes of the K-12 curriculum in physical education.
3. Obtain evidence about what various groups of individuals (experts) think are the most important outcomes to be acquired as a result of the K-12 school curriculum in physical education. Include opinions of:
   a. professional physical educators
   b. parents of students (past, present, future)
   c. school administrators (building, central)
   d. community leaders (board members, others)
   e. students (past, present, future)
4. Identify the goals of an exemplary physical education program that can be directly linked to the documented contributions and/or outcomes that are highly valued.
5. Identify specific content (at the program objective level) that operationally defines the K-12 goals.
6. Identify the criteria and standards of performance that operationally define program objectives.
7. Prioritize the relative importance of the defined objectives.
8. Estimate the amount of instructional time needed to have a majority of students achieve the level of mastery defined in "6" above.
   a. the initial levels of fitness, skill, knowledge, values
   b. if significant changes in performance or behavior have occurred as a result of the program's intervention
9. Using the estimates of needed instructional time, available instructional time, other resources (staff, equipment, facilities), and objective priorities, identify the program objectives that will be taught at each grade level.
10. Obtain (develop/select/alter) the instructional materials and procedures designed to improve student performance on the selected objectives.
11. Implement, evaluate, and report the effectiveness of the program.
12. Revise the materials and procedures as needed to improve their effectiveness and/or efficiency, re-implement, and re-evaluate.

Figure 2.4. Steps for developing an exemplary program

schooling, and change, the physical education program is planned, implemented, evaluated, and refined.

The model facilitates a strong correspondence between the evaluation of program outcomes, the goals and objectives that specify program intent, and the literature that documents their appropriateness. Similarly, the model provides for an evaluation process which requires the program to be sufficiently described so that it can be systematically improved in terms of effectiveness and efficiency. This description permits the program's transfer to other sites where teachers and administrators wish to implement the program's materials or procedures.

OVERVIEW OF THE STEPS INVOLVED IN PROGRAM IMPROVEMENT

The steps used to develop or redefine a physical education program are listed in Figure 2-4.

Review of the steps in Figure 2-4 will reveal a strong relationship between the steps and the remaining chapters of this book. This relationship is illustrated below.

Steps to Program Improvement	Chapter
1. Identify contributions of physical activity to well-being	3
2. Convert contributions to program outcomes	4
3. Obtain estimates of relative importance of the outcomes	4
4. Identify appropriate program goals	4
5. Identify program objectives	5
6. Identify instructional objectives	5
7. Prioritize relative importance of program objectives	6
8. Estimate instructional time needed	6
9. Organize the program content K-12	6
10. Develop instructional materials	7, 8
11. Implement and evaluate the program	9, 10
12. Revise and re-implement the program	9, 10

As indicated in Chapter 10, devoted to Program Evaluation, the appropriate way to determine if the materials and procedures described in this book are relevant to program improvement in a specific setting is to conduct a self-study of the school district. Self-study procedures are described in Chapter 10, and a self-study instrument is included in Appendix C. A brief alternative to conducting a self-study would be to compare the characteristics of the program of interest with the criteria for program evaluation included in Appendix A and illustrated in Figure 2-1. When criteria are not met in a convincing manner, it may be helpful to consider the remaining chapters of the book for assistance in redirecting the program.

Chapter 3

Contributions of Physical Activity to Well-Being

The benefits of physical activity to mental and physical health are numerous and varied. Fortunately, these benefits apply to the entire population, whether infant, child, adolescent, or adult. There is also abundant evidence that early and consistent exposure to the appropriate kinds and amounts of activity has a cumulative effect, thereby allowing children of school ages to gain the experiences that may eliminate or postpone the destructive forces that accompany inactive lifestyles.

Although the benefits of physical activity have been known for many years, the evidence has not been systematically accumulated or condensed until the present time. This evidence is available for those who wish to review this compelling accumulation in its entirety (Seefeldt, 1986). Those who wish to read a condensed version of the documented evidence relating physical activity to well-being will find *The Value of Physical Activity* (Seefeldt and Vogel, 1986) to be helpful. Despite this condensation, the information is still too extensive for inclusion in a document such as this. Therefore, in this document we have divided the content of *Physical Activity and Well-Being* into five categories, and have provided a brief overview about the kinds of statements to be found in the original sources. These categories are represented by 20 statements included in Appendix D. The extent to which these outcomes have been achieved in organized physical education programs is recorded in Appendix E.

CATEGORIES OF OUTCOMES ASSOCIATED WITH PHYSICAL ACTIVITY

Motor Skill Acquisition

The voluntary motor skills that underlie the abilities to perform the sports, games, and dances of our culture are learned most efficiently during infancy and childhood and continue to be refined during adolescence and adulthood. Competence in the fundamental skills of locomotion, projection, and reception is the base from which the integration of skills occurs. Children who develop a variety of movement skills are able to call on these experiences when they are learning new skills. The broad base of fundamental movement skills also permits them to approach new skills with greater confidence.

Physical Growth and Maturation

The stresses of normal physical activity and even those of strenuous training do not seem to adversely affect the rates of physical growth or maturation. However, the assessment of growth and maturity are important because size and biological age are closely related to the motor capacities of the body. Conversely, physical activity does have a distinct influence on the structure of bones and the size and strength of muscles, tendons, and ligaments. Physical activity also plays a major role in the maintenance of normal body weight and the reduction of fat tissue.

Health-related Fitness

Perhaps the outcomes that are most easily demonstrated through physical education programs are associated with health-related fitness. Recent attempts to identify the components of health-related fitness generally include an assessment of cardiorespiratory function, body fat, strength of the back and stomach muscles, and flexibility. All of these components can be modified in positive ways through systematic programs of activity, both for students and adults. The health-related benefits of physical activity provide a compelling argument for its inclusion in the school curriculum. The prospect of delaying or abetting such problems as atherosclerotic diseases, obesity, diabetes, and osteoporosis, and increasing functional capacity in muscular strength and endurance, anaerobic and aerobic power, flexibility, and agility, are all persuasive reasons for advocating good programs of physical education.

Skilled Performance

One of the most powerful motivators for continuing an active lifestyle in adulthood is related to having experienced such an environment during childhood and adolescence. Adults are more likely to engage in activities with which they are familiar and feel adequately skilled. These reasons suggest that if we are to prepare adults for a lifetime of activity, then the base must relate to the fundamental skills of childhood, which have had an opportunity to become refined and integrated into selected games, dances, and sports of adolescence and adulthood.

Mental, Social, and Moral Development

Opportunities for positive mental, social, and moral development exist in physical education programs. However, evidence indicates that unless these experiences are deliberately incorporated into the structure of activities and their desirable outcomes sought, undesirable outcomes are just as likely to occur.

Infants and children often use movement as a vehicle for their mental and social development. The inquisitive nature of children is often satisfied by the ability to walk, run, crawl, climb, or jump to otherwise inaccessible sites where objects or events have aroused their curiosity. Children who do not move efficiently lack these early opportunities, and in later childhood they may become socially isolated because of deficiencies in movement skills as perceived by themselves or peers.

Delay of Aging

The benefits of physical activity are dramatically noted in aged individuals, first, when their former capacity to move diminishes, but just as remarkably, when a program involving rehabilitation is initiated. Numerous investigators have produced evidence that physical activity is able to forestall the debilitating effects of old age. The beneficial effects of activity in elderly individuals is manifested in the following areas: mental health, self-concept, cardiovascular function, blood pressure, non-insulin and insulin-dependent diabetes, and low-back pain. Although there is little evidence that physical activity will increase one's life span, there is abundant evidence that it can enhance the quality of life.

Chapter 4

Development of Relevant and Defensible Goals

RATIONALE FOR COMMUNITY INVOLVEMENT

By converting the scientific literature which enumerates contributions of activity to the quality of life (identified in Chapter 3) into a series of statements that can be rated, it is possible to obtain an estimate of what community representatives value as the most important elements of a physical education program. There are several important reasons for taking this action.

1. The physical education staff can communicate many documented benefits of physical activity to representatives of the community, who control the resources used to support physical education. Community representatives are often amazed at the potential that exists within physical education to influence their children in a positive way.

2. By asking community representatives for information regarding the benefits they believe are most important for their children, the staff obtains an indication of which outcomes are perceived as most relevant. Such information adds credibility to the program goals and objectives which have been stated to represent the contributions of physical activity to the welfare of the students.

3. A third, and perhaps the most important outcome of obtaining community input, is the base of support that is developed for the program and the process used to improve the program. Another important result is that ownership of the program is extended beyond the physical education staff to representatives of the community.

By obtaining ratings of the relative importance of potential physical education outcomes, the project staff can establish goals and objectives that are consistent with 1) what can be acquired in physical education programs (defensible in terms of scientific evidence) and 2) the values the community holds as important for its children (relevant).

ASSIGNING IMPORTANCE TO THE CONTRIBUTIONS

As indicated above, identifying the contributions of physical activity to well-being should be followed by obtaining community input regarding their relative importance. This can be accomplished in a two-hour meeting where the potential contributions and how they will be used in designing or redesigning the K-12 program are clearly communicated. A community advisory committee representing central administration, building-level representatives, physical education and classroom teachers from all curriculum levels, parents from all levels, secondary students, and others whose judgment is valued should be invited to participate.

The meeting agenda should include:

1. Welcome and introductions
2. Purpose of the meeting
3. Review of the curriculum improvement project
   a. Need for program improvement
   b. Procedural steps
   c. Anticipated outcomes
4. Presentation of the contributions of physical activity to well-being
5. Rating the relative importance of the contributions of physical activity to well-being
6. Review of the next steps to be taken to improve the physical education curriculum.

Review of the Curriculum Development Process

After the welcome and introductions of those present, it is important to state the purpose of the meeting and to review the curriculum improvement project. The need for program improvement should be clearly communicated. This can be accomplished best if it has been well defined by completing a self-study of the program referred to in Chapters 2 and 10 in accordance with the Self-Study Checklist included in Appendix C. The graphic report format incorporated in the Self-Study Checklist is particularly conducive to helping communicate areas of need.

After clarifying the need, the anticipated products and the procedures by which the products will be developed should be communicated. The information contained in Chapter 2, Figure 2-1, and Figure 2-4 provides the content to be covered here.

Present the Contributions of Physical Activity to Well-being

The contributions of physical activity to well-being should be clearly communicated to the community advisory group. Using the handout provided in Appendix D, indicate that all the infor-

Development of Relevant and Defensible Goals

mation included on the handout comes from the primary source, *Physical Activity and Well-Being*, and note that its contents have scientific validity. It may be helpful to supplement the information in Appendix D with a second handout of information included in Chapter 3. Distribute the instrument for rating the relative importance of the various statements (see Appendix F) and explain that it is another revision of the statements included in Appendix D designed to obtain information that reveals the community's values regarding the relative importance of the various contribution statements.

Rate the Relative Importance of the Various Statements that Associate Physical Activity to Well-being

This is the primary portion of the meeting. The recommended procedure is to have each person independently rate the relative importance of each item. When the initial ratings are completed, the person conducting the meeting should ask individuals who rated a specific item high to share their reasons. This same request should then be made of those who rated the item low. Other reasons that have not been communicated are then requested from persons who recorded high, low, or moderate ratings. A three- to seven-minute time limit is placed on the discussion for each item, after which the item is re-rated by all members of the group. This procedure clarifies terminology, provides an opportunity for illustrative examples, and reveals the important reasons why each item should be rated high or low. The process provides a complete base of information for the advisory group before participants complete the re-ratings. Re-ratings are then averaged to represent the relative importance assigned to the potential contributions.

STATING APPROPRIATE PROGRAM GOALS

The terms *goals* and *objectives* have been used in so many different ways and at so many different levels of specificity that the terms no longer have precision. Goals, as the term is used here, refers to a broad general statement of program intent. Objectives are more specific statements that describe what students will be able to do after instruction. As a general statement of program intent, a goal represents large but unique portions of curricular content. Because program goals and objectives should indicate the "results" of the things we do during the program's implementation, it is critical that the goals meet at least three criteria. These criteria are:

1. The goals must be defensible in terms of the potential outcomes they represent.

2. They should reflect the values of members of the local community.

3. They should be stated in output terminology, and should suggest levels of performance that are expected from the students.

Criteria one and two are easily met when the goals are written to represent the contributions of activity to well-being and when these contributions have been rated by members of the community. The third criterion requires that the goals are appropriately stated.

Stating goals in "output" rather than "input" terminology serves to focus the program on the outcomes or results of instruction, rather than on inputs to the instructional process. Three key terms are common to such goal statements. The term "demonstrate" is a useful component of the goal statement because its presence requires students who have met the goal to attain some observable outcome. The term "competence" is appropriate for similar reasons because it suggests that an identifiable level of performance must be stated. The term "selected" indicates that specific program content must be specified. An example of the appropriate use of these terms would be "to demonstrate competence in selected fundamental motor skills."

An example of a goal statement in which incorrect or "input" terminology is used would be "to provide the students with an opportunity to learn fundamental motor skills." Technically, this goal could be met with one period of instruction focusing on the fundamental motor skills. However, there would be no indication of whether or not the students achieved competence in the skills.

Another consideration when stating program goals is their level of specificity. Sample curricular content commonly includes four broad categories: affective characteristics, cognitive skills, fitness capacities, and motor skills. Accordingly, the potential contributions of activity when converted to program goals could be stated for the four broad categories of content or for more discrete subdivisions of those areas.

The level of specificity of goal statements should be considered a matter of local preference because the broad and narrow goal statements must be clearly operationalized through the identification of objectives in order to adequately define their meanings. A broad goal, therefore, would merely contain more objectives than a more narrowly stated goal. Examples of goal statements progressing from general to specific include:

1. Demonstrate competence in selected motor skills
2. Demonstrate competence in selected fundamental motor skills
3. Demonstrate competence in selected fundamental object control skills

Broadly stated goals quickly communicate program content and narrowly stated goals provide visibility to more discrete portions of program content. Regardless of the choice to state broad or narrow goals, both must be operationalized with clearly stated program objectives.

As suggested above, there are many ways that program goals can be stated to relate the contributions of physical activity to well-being. One such account is included in Figure 4-1.

Developing defensible, relevant, and appropriately stated goals is an important step in the curriculum improvement process. The roots and rationale for the goals should provide a source of confidence in the program's direction to the school district's administration and staff. It has been our experience that when the steps suggested in this chapter have been implemented, confidence in program direction has resulted.

1. To demonstrate competence in selected fundamental motor skills

2. To demonstrate competence in selected lifetime sports, games and activities

3. To demonstrate knowledge of selected cognitive concepts

4. To demonstrate competence in selected body control skills

5. To demonstrate competence on selected indicators of physical fitness

6. To demonstrate competence in selected sport-related personal, social, and attitudinal skills

Figure 4.1. Example goals of physical education

Chapter 5

Development of Program and Instructional Objectives

Goals, program objectives, and instructional objectives are necessary to clearly communicate the intended results of instruction. The ability to clearly specify objectives is important in several areas:

1. Selecting content
2. Sequencing content
3. Delivering effective instruction
4. Evaluating the effects and efficiency of instruction.

Two steps are necessary in order to complete the transition from goals to student levels of performance:

1. Operationalize each goal by identifying the program objectives that, when obtained, would indicate that the goals have been achieved.
2. Define each program objective by identifying the instructional objectives that indicate achievement of the program objectives.

IDENTIFYING PROGRAM OBJECTIVES

The term "program objectives" is used to describe elements of program content. Program objectives consist of a few words or often a single word and only have precise meaning when they are operationally defined by their associated instructional objectives.

Examples of program objectives for a goal associated with the fundamental motor skills are illustrated in Figure 5-1. Program objectives, as illustrated here, are purposely simplified to allow them to be used efficiently during the process of organizing the curriculum within and across grades, as illustrated in Chapter 6. Competence on each program objective is defined by the last instructional objective in the sequence, as will be illustrated in the next section of this chapter.

The task of operationalizing each goal by specifying program objectives requires identification of the skills, knowledges, fitness capacities, and affective characteristics that would be acceptable as evidence that the goal has been attained by graduates of the program. As illustrated in Figure 5-1, the fundamental motor skills that were "selected" (using the key term in the goal

> **Example Goal: To Demonstrate Competence on Selected Fundamental Motor Skills**
>
> Divisions of Goal Content:
>
> Program Objectives:
>
> | Locomotor Skills | Object Control Skills |
> |---|---|
> | Run | Underhand Roll |
> | Leap | Underhand Throw |
> | Horizontal Jump | Overhand Throw |
> | Vertical Jump | Kick |
> | Hop | Catch |
> | Gallop | Underhand Strike |
> | Slide | Forehand Strike |
> | Skip | Backhand Strike |
> | | Sidearm Strike |

Figure 5.1. Example program objectives

statement) are listed. The degree to which the students obtain competence (another key term) is the degree to which the goals will be obtained.

Appendix G provides many examples of program objectives that can be used to operationalize goals commonly used in programs of physical education. The appendix includes the following material.

1. Six goals, stated in "outcome" terminology
2. Program objectives that can be used to operationalize each goal
3. Several rationales why the goal and its program objectives should be included in programs of physical education
4. Criteria that can be used to select or prioritize the program objectives within each goal

IDENTIFICATION OF INSTRUCTIONAL OBJECTIVES

Instructional objectives define the performance levels that students must attain to achieve the program objectives, and ultimately, the goals of the program. They should be written to represent levels of student ability that range from the lowest levels of incompetence to competence on the program objective. Each instructional objective should be written to clearly describe student performance levels so that teachers are able to determine if students have achieved the intended performance levels.

Two or more instructional objectives are usually associated with each program objective, depending on student needs, teacher preference, or reporting needs. As with the specificity of goal statements, there is a trade-off when stating instructional objectives at two or many levels of specificity. Two levels simplifies the objective-writing, implementation, and reporting process but restricts the frequency with which students' gains in competence can be reported. Ten levels would improve the ability to report students' gains in performance but would complicate the writing and use of the instructional objectives. The important choice is to clearly specify instructional objectives that define what will be accepted as evidence of having attained the objective. The number of instructional objectives per program objective is largely one of preference. In this document, we have chosen to use two instructional objectives for each program objective.

An example of a program objective for the overhand throw and its two instructional objectives is included in Figure 5-2. Instructional Objective 1 is qualitative because it seeks to focus early instruction on correct throwing form. Correct form is operationally defined by the key elements of form described as a, b, c, d, and e. Most physical educators will agree that achievement of these key elements of form are prerequisite to attaining one's individual potential in throwing for distance and accuracy. Yet, it is common for instruction and assessment of performance ability to be driven by criteria based on distance and accuracy. Accordingly, the talented, large, or early maturing child who achieves high scores for distance and accuracy relative to peers may be deceived into thinking that he or she is a competent thrower. Consequently, this child may never obtain his or her potential due to deficiencies in form that were ignored because of relatively good scores in quantitative performance.

PROGRAM OBJECTIVE: OVERHAND THROW

Instructional Objective 1

Demonstrate appropriate throwing form two consecutive times.
  a. Side orientation to initiate the throw
  b. Weight transfer to the foot opposite the throwing arm as the throwing arm passes the shoulder
  c. Hip, followed by shoulder, rotation during the throwing motion
  d. Arm action initiated with a near complete downward extension of the arm (hand on top of the ball)
  e. Hand passes above and outside of the shoulder

Instructional Objective 2

Maintain appropriate throwing form and hit a six-foot-square target placed one foot above the ground from a distance of 40 feet, two consecutive times.

Figure 5.2. Example program and instructional objectives

After achieving the elements of acceptable or mature form, Instructional Objective 2 refocuses instruction on maintaining form while adding criteria for distance and accuracy. The criteria selected (size of target and distance of the throw) are written indicators of what the staff is willing to accept as evidence of successful achievement of the objective. Accordingly, Instructional Objective 2 operationally defines the level of performance necessary to obtain competence on the program objective.

The relationship between the two instructional objectives for each program objective and the instructional activities, is illustrated in Figure 5-3. Instructional Objective 1 provides the criterion for dividing students into two performance levels: those who have not yet acquired the elements of form and those who have. Instructional Objective 2 adds the criterion for another level of student performance; it is for those students who have achieved the stated criteria for distance and accuracy. Instructional materials are planned and instruction is implemented to move students from one performance level to the next.

Objective-Related Instructional Activities

Program Objective: To demonstrate competence on the overhand throw

Instructional Objectives	Student Performance Levels	Instructional Activities
	1. Inappropriate form	
1. Appropriate form		
	2. Appropriate form	One or more teaching learning activities, games, and/or drills designed to facilitate student achievement of the next performance level
2. Appropriate form plus functional ability		
	3. Form plus function	

Note that the performance criteria of Instructional Objective 1 divides students into two categories [i.e., those with inappropriate form (✓-) and those with appropriate form (✓).] Similarly, Instructional Objective 2 further divides students into those that have achieved the form performance criteria of Instructional Objective 1 (✓) and those who have achieved distance and/or accuracy criteria (✓+)

Figure 5.3. The relationship between instructional objectives, student performance, and instructional activities

Figure 5-4 provides an example of this two-level format for instructional objectives for a physical fitness program objective. For the program objective aerobic fitness, Instructional Objective 1 defines a specific level of fitness to be obtained, and Instructional Level 2 specifies that the desired level must be maintained for an extended period of time. Initial levels and periods of time, as with the criteria for distance and accuracy in the previous example, can be modified as deemed appropriate in local districts. Again, there are many additional divisions that could be used, but the preference here is to keep all instructional objectives in the two-level format for consistency and ease of communication to others.

PROGRAM OBJECTIVE: AEROBIC FITNESS

Instructional Objective #1:

Demonstrate an appropriate level of aerobic fitness by completing the one-mile run at or above the 75th percentile on national norms for peers of the same age and gender

Instructional Objective #2:

Maintain the above listed level of aerobic fitness over three consecutive six-week marking periods

---

Figure 5.4. Example program and instructional objective for physical fitness

Similarly, program and instructional objectives for cognitive and affective achievement can be stated at two instructional levels. For cognitive objectives, Instructional Level 1 objectives have been written that specify what information is to be understood, while Level 2 Instructional Objectives specify competence in the application of the Level 1 information. Affective instructional objectives at Level 1 describe the attainment of selected affective characteristics, while Instructional Level 2 describes their maintenance without additional intervention or control by the instructor.

Instructional objectives are critical to the entire objective-related instructional process. Without clear specification of the intended results of instruction, it is difficult to effectively design instruction or to evaluate the results of instruction.

> **PROGRAM OBJECTIVE: EFFECTS OF EXERCISE**
>
> **Instructional Objective 1**
>
> Demonstrate knowledge of the effects of exercise in the following areas (80 percent mastery of associated knowledge test):
>
> a. Aerobic/anaerobic energy production
> b. Muscular fitness - endurance, strength, power, and flexibility
> c. Growth and development
> d. General physical health benefits
> e. General mental and social health benefits
> f. Skill and knowledge of physical activity
> g. Exercise myths and contraindicated exercises
>
> **Instructional Objective 2**
>
> Demonstrate the ability to apply the knowledge included in Instructional Objective 1 (a-g) to the development of a personalized sequential program of activities designed to obtain and maintain the beneficial effects of exercise (80 percent mastery of the "application" criteria).

Figure 5.5. Example program and instructional objectives for the cognitive program area

Chapter 6

Organization of the K-12 Curriculum

Many of the criticisms of physical education programs relate to their organization. Among the common complaints are lack of sequential progressions, redundancy of instruction, too much or too little content, activities unrelated to goals and objectives, content placed at inappropriate grade levels, and units that are too long or too short. All of these problems are difficult to resolve without a specified curriculum structure that can be systematically modified in accordance with information derived from evaluation, changes in instructional procedures, or alterations in the objectives of instruction.

Several important points must be considered when attempting to develop an appropriate K-12 structure. Of primary importance are the following:

1. The curriculum structure must represent the best thinking of the entire K-12 staff.

2. School districts do not have sufficient resources, staff, time, equipment, and facilities to include all possible content in their K-12 programs. Accordingly, the discrepancy between resources needed and resources available must be systematically resolved.

3. Because all possible objectives cannot be incorporated in the program, objectives must be prioritized. Those considered most important must be included in the early versions of the program.

4. Objectives selected for inclusion in the program must be sequentially placed in grades where instruction can be most effectively delivered.

5. Organization of the objectives within grade levels requires at least three types of instructional units.

PROCEDURES FOR DEVELOPING A CURRICULUM STRUCTURE

The development or redirection of the curriculum must involve all members of the K-12 physical education staff. This process is most effective when administrators and parents are also involved. A consultant, familiar with the procedures outlined in this book, is necessary to keep the individuals involved from getting bogged down in the many diversions that can occur in the redirection process.

All participants cannot, however, be involved in all aspects of the redirection process. Rather, a Work Committee that includes a representative of each curriculum level and at least one central administrator is necessary to generate the prototype materials and procedures which is then presented for the review and reaction of the others involved. For example, in large school districts the full physical education staff, the community advisory group, administrative councils, and/or a Work Committee of eight to 12 individuals should be involved to generate the curriculum prototype. The Work Committee or group representatives must accomplish the following five tasks:

1. Select program objectives that operationalize the goals derived from the potential contributions of physical activity to well-being. The program objectives must appropriately represent the ratings of relative importance of those contributions.

2. Identify the grade levels where it is most appropriate to provide instruction on each stated program objective.

3. Estimate the amount of instructional time needed within each grade level to teach each objective so that a specified percentage of the students (at least 75 percent) achieve the intended levels of competence.

4. Resolve the discrepancy between instructional time needed and instructional time available by selecting a core of program objectives that has the highest priority among those available.

5. Organize the program objectives within grade levels to facilitate effectiveness and efficiency of instruction.

Selecting Program Objectives for Inclusion in the Curriculum

Appendix H provides a worksheet for identifying the program objectives that should be included in the program to fully operationalize each program goal. Completion of this task provides an indication of the content that should be included in a fully funded physical education program appropriate for the given school district. There should be a direct relationship between the program objectives selected, the stated goals, and the contributions of physical activity to well-being that received high ratings from the community advisory group.

The selection process can be accomplished by having members of the Work Committee independently circle the numbers of the program objectives they believe are essential. The individual selections are then compiled to form a composite from the Work Committee. At this point all program objectives selected by two or more members of the Work Committee should be included for consideration in the curriculum.

Completion of this step results in the compilation of program objectives, by goal, that the Work Committee believes should be included in the K-12 physical education program. It is a prototype of what should be in place. It can be anticipated, however, that more program objectives will be selected than can be effectively taught within available resources. Although not all identified objectives can be taught, it remains important, however, to identify them (program objectives) as content that *should* be included in the program to fully achieve the stated goals.

Because the program objectives included at each level have not been reduced in number to appropriately fit the amount of instructional time available, the program must be considered "ideal," and not necessarily "real." It is important, however, that the objectives selected for inclusion in the program not be restricted at this point by time, equipment, or staffing patterns. This formulation of an ideal rather than a realistic program is not a limitation but a strength, because the process identifies the type of program that the community has indicated should be available to students. Subsequent reference to this ideal physical education program will be valuable as additional resources necessary to add content to the program are sought. As indicated earlier, these requests should be made only when there is convincing evidence of effectiveness in achieving a reduced number of high priority objectives.

Placement of Objectives at Appropriate Grade Levels

After identifying a composite of program objectives that will serve to comprehensively operationalize stated program goals, the placements of program objectives by grade level should be made. Be assured that no matter what placements are made, students in every grade level will represent the full range in ability defined by the instructional objectives of each program objective. Dramatic shifts in performance levels should occur, however, with effective instruction across grade levels. For example, if instruction on the overhand throw is scheduled to begin in kindergarten and end in grade five, we would expect 75 percent or more of the kindergarten students to be below the level of competence described in instructional objectives, whereas at grade five we would expect 75 percent or more of the students to achieve Instructional Objective 2, which specifies the additional criteria of distance and accuracy which must accompany the demonstration of mature form—the requirement of Instructional Objective 1. Grades two through four would have students exhibiting relatively balanced mixes of competence on the objective.

It is not practical to expect that all children will achieve the specified level of competence in throwing, catching, and batting, but it is practical to expect that with clear objectives and effective instruction over several years, major shifts in competence will occur. If stated objectives are not achieved and graduates of our programs do not gain these competencies, something is radically wrong. Accordingly, the Work Committee members must pool their best thinking and identify the grades wherein it is most appropriate to teach the specified levels of competence. These judgments are difficult because they are somewhat subjective in nature and are not based on well-defined criteria. Nonetheless, they must be made and systematically altered as more is learned about instructional practices and the capabilities of students in specific instructional settings.

The portion of Appendix H included under Curriculum Level should be completed for each program objective that is included in the curriculum. These determinations should be made individually by the Work Committee members (a check in the appropriate space is sufficient) and then summarized to form a composite, based on a discussion of the rationale supporting the various points of view. The determination of grade placement for specific objectives includes a tendency to extend the same program objectives across many grade levels. This inclination should be avoided, however, because it prolongs the instruction on most program objectives into the high school years. It is much better to limit the time in which instruction occurs to four to six years of concentrated teaching and thus determine the degree to which instruction is effective.

Assignment of Instructional Time to Objectives

The next step in the curriculum organizational process involves estimating the amount of instructional time needed to effectively teach each program objective. Many programs are ineffective because teachers attempt to teach too much content. Often the amount of available time is simply divided by the number of program objectives that have been identified. The consequence of this approach is that insufficient amounts of instructional time are assigned to each objective, resulting in insignificant student achievements.

The assignment of insufficient instructional time is one explanation for the historic complaints of high school and junior high school teachers' concerning the low performance levels of students who come to them from the elementary and junior high school programs. Yet, this dilemma is created, in part, by attempting to teach too many objectives in the time that is available.

The determination of available instructional time is easily accomplished. Simply count the number of days that are available for instruction and multiply the days by the length of each instructional period. For example, schools commonly are in session for six periods of six weeks, or 36 weeks for the entire school year. If the physical education class meets three times a week for 30 minutes each class period, the available instructional time is 36 weeks times three periods/week times 30 minutes, or 3240 minutes.

Those who have taught in the public schools, however, realize that such an estimate of available time is much too liberal. The calculation must be adjusted to account for "lost" instructional days that occur as a result of fire drills, assemblies, snow or storm days, and student field trips. Experience has shown that in most instances this loss will be nearly 10 percent of the available time. The 3240 minutes should, therefore, be reduced (3240 times .90 = 2916 or slightly over 46 1/2 hours) in anticipation of the interruptions.

The determination of needed instructional time is more complex than the calculation of available time. The reason for the complexity is that the estimate obtained is a function of two other considerations. The first requires a decision regarding how much individual student gain is sufficient to be labeled as meaningful. The second builds on the first and requires a decision regarding the number of students (percentage) within a class or program level who must achieve the criterion of individual student gain in order to meet the goals of the program.

Meaningful gain refers to that amount of performance gain that is judged to be educationally important. It must be large enough to make a difference in the student's ability to demonstrate a significantly higher level of competence on the objective. Gains must be sufficiently large so that their accumulation within the allotted instructional time results in the desirable level of competence as stated in the instructional objectives.

A second consideration for identifying needed instructional time is based on the number (*e.g.*, 75 percent) of students targeted to achieve competence in each objective. If the program seeks to have 90 percent of the students achieving competence on 90 percent of the program's objectives, more instructional time will be necessary than if the program seeks to have 50 percent of the students gain competence on 50 percent of the objectives. When the number targeted to achieve competence is determined, all estimates of instructional time needed should be made in accordance with this criterion.

Based upon the experience of the staff and the expected levels of performance of the students, the amount of time assigned to each objective can be determined. Some program objectives will require more time, while others will require less. It is not critical that the estimate be precise. It is critical, however, that an estimate of the required time be made. The estimate will be modified during the implementation and evaluation of the program, in accordance with more information about how much students are able to achieve within specific times.

The estimates should be completed individually and then collectively by members of the Work Committee. An example of estimates completed is included in Figure 6-1. The 90 in the K- six columns indicates that 90 minutes of instruction will be devoted to teaching the program during the specified grade levels. This time may be divided into six 15-minute instructional episodes, nine 10-minute episodes, 18 five-minute episodes, or some combination of these time allocations.

After completing the estimates of needed time for each program objective, the estimates should be summed both within and across grades. Totals across grades for each program objective should be viewed for their sensibility and altered as needed. Ask and answer the question: "Is the specified amount of instructional time appropriate (too little or too much) to develop the level of competence identified in the last instructional objective for the specified number (75 percent) of students?" If the collective experience of the Work Committee members indicates that the allocated time is inappropriate, then it should be enhanced or reduced as necessary.

Selection, Placement and Estimation of Needed Instructional Time for a Sample of Program Objectives

Curriculum Levels

PROGRAM OBJECTIVES	K	1	2	3	4	5	6	7	8	9	10
1. To demonstrate competence in selected fundamental motor skills.											
overhand throw	90	90	90	90	90						
underhand roll	90	90	90	90							
underhand throw	90	90	90	90	90						
dribble (feet)	90	90	90	90	90						
dribble (hands)		90	90	90	90						
catch (flys)		90	90	90	90	90					
catch (grounders)	90	90	90	90	90						
forehand strike			90	90	90	90	90				
batting		90	90	90	90	90					
kick		90	90	90	90	90					
punt		90	90	90	90	90					
vertical jump		90	90	90	90	90					
horizontal jump		90	90	90	90	90					
run	90	90	90	90	90						
slide	90	90	90								
gallop	90	90	90	90							
hop	90	90	90	90							
skip	90	90	90	90							
rope jump	90	90	90	90							
TOTALS											
minutes	900	1620	1620	1530	1170	60	90				
hours	15.0	27.0	27.0	25.5	19.5	6	1.5				

Figure 6.1. Example estimates of needed instructional time

Summing the time allocated for objectives within each grade provides an estimate of the time needed to develop competence in the objectives that should be included in the K-12 program.

Typically, this calculation results in numbers that are much larger than the time available for instruction. The size of the discrepancy is usually a good indication of a difficulty common to most programs of physical education. As physical educators we typically attempt to develop competence in far more objectives than is possible within time constraints. As a result, most of the graduates of our required programs are exposed to many objectives but gain competence in few of them. To the degree that this occurs, we fuel the fire of discontent, resulting in the erosion of support for our programs because many students, administrators, and parents believe that students are not achieving significant outcomes in physical education.

Determining the Number of Objectives to Teach

The determination of how many objectives can be included in the program can be made by comparing the amount of time needed for the selected program objectives with the total amount of time available. Without such a comparison, it is fully predictable that too many objectives will be included in the program. A large number of program objectives may be impressive on paper when communicating the program's content to others. However, communicating the results of instruction to administrators, legislators, parents, and/or board members under these circumstances can be disastrous.

Physical educators must be able to demonstrate that a difference in student competencies is occurring as a result of their participation in the program. There must be a good match between the resources available and scope of the program. This match can only occur when priorities that identify the most important program objectives are invoked during the process of selecting content. The amount of content that can be included in the program simply must be based on the match between time available for instruction and time needed for a significant number of students to achieve functional competence on selected objectives.

Prioritization of the program objectives can also be recorded on the form in Appendix H. Again, the process to develop the priorities should use individual ratings of the Work Committee, followed by limited discussion of the rationale for ratings that are at variance, followed by re-rating and calculating a final rating based on consensus. Appendix H includes two columns under the heading Priority. The first column can be used for the initial rating and the second for the rating subsequent to a group discussion. A composite rating for each objective should be calculated, and then the entire list should be dated and bear the names of the group members who determined the ratings.

Ratings of all program objectives on a one to five point scale (or its equivalent) can be used to complete the prioritization task. This approach is simple but it tends to result in relatively high ratings and, therefore insignificant differences between many objectives. The small differences between objectives tend to decrease the usefulness of this technique as a process to reduce the content of programs. An alternative method that results in a better spread of objectives is a "priority selection" approach. This approach is implemented by having the Work Committee select a number of top priority objectives (*e.g.*, 20) and assign them the number five. When this is completed, they identify the next lower priority set of 20 objectives and assign them the number four. This is repeated for sets of 20 that are assigned the numbers three, two, and one. Following discussion of the rationales and an opportunity for re-selection, the numbers are consolidated and the final priorities calculated.

When priorities have been established for the program objectives, the Work Committee can systematically resolve the time available—time needed discrepancies in program content. This must be completed within each grade level by selecting the number of priority objectives that account for the amount of time available. The committee must also be sensitive to objectives included in prior and subsequent grade levels that are prerequisites or related in some important way to the objectives being selected at each grade level.

Because the identification of objectives and the estimates of time are prototypes for an organizational structure that will be refined subsequent to being taught in selected grades by selected teachers, it is recommended that the number of program objectives included in the prototype represent a "core" of approximately 75 percent of the available instructional time. This allows needed flexibility for anticipated time overruns and also allows some flexibility for teachers to incorporate content that they believe is important but which did not achieve a priority status.

Prioritizing the program's objectives results in including those objectives considered to be most important. What about the objectives that are important but that were eliminated from the program? Typically, teachers are very resistant to excluding them; they feel the students are being short-changed if some of the content that was taught previously is eliminated by this new approach. However, exercising the alternative of reinstating the excessive program objectives only worsens the situation. If time estimates are correct and instruction is effective, then students will make significant improvements on a selected group of high-priority objectives. If available time is overloaded by excessive program objectives, few students will make meaningful gains.

Another way to view the program objectives that are important but not of sufficient priority to be included in the program is to treat them as a primary rationale for requesting increases in program resources (time, equipment, facilities, staffing). The reduction of program content to include only high-priority program objectives, based upon appropriate time allotments, provides an opportunity to demonstrate that the program is effective on high-priority objectives within given resources. You can also show that other content was identified as important but had to be excluded due to limited resources. In this way, there is a direct link between program content and resources. Reductions in staff, time, equipment, and/or facilities will cause reduction in program content; increases in these same resources will result in additional student outcomes. In this way, administrators understand the impact of their decisions about resources. In a very real sense, the program objectives that were not included in the curriculum became the rationale for requesting increased resource allocations. The more high-priority program objectives that must be cut to achieve effectiveness, the stronger the rationale for increased allotments of resources. The process that has been described emphasizes effectiveness within existing resource constraints and establishes a strong base for requesting additional resources to meet additional program objectives.

Organization of Program Objectives Within Grade Levels

After the program objectives have been identified for each level of the program, they must be organized for instructional purposes. Typically, there is a September to June sequence of instructional units. Instructional units are typically made up of clusters of program objectives that have been grouped together for teaching purposes.

Unless there is district-wide scheduling of units to facilitate sharing of equipment or facilities, the teaching sequence within grade levels should be the prerogative of each teacher. There are, however, three basic types of instructional units that teachers can use for instructional planning. They are defined here as "traditional," "long-term," and "continuous."

Traditional units are those that cluster several program objectives together into a unit that is taught over a period of approximately one to five weeks, with the typical length being two to three weeks. Examples of this type of units are those commonly used to teach swimming, soccer, and/or object control.

Long-term units are clusters of program objectives that are taught over extended periods of time, ranging from six to 36 weeks. These units are taught simultaneously with other units because they consume only small portions of time within each lesson. A typical example is a fitness unit that emphasizes a cluster of fitness program objectives taught, conducted, and/or monitored within the teaching of program objectives in other units.

A continuous unit refers to the conscious, but intermittent, teaching of program objectives that are not specifically scheduled for particular points in time, but rather are taught when the appropriate circumstances occur. This type of unit is typified by program objectives in the affective area. Cooperation, self-control, respect for others, and best effort are examples of program objectives that are included in a "continuous" unit. Although we may not contrive situations to facilitate instruction in these important areas, they constantly occur in competitive and interactive circumstances. Because the need for positive feedback is great, they therefore merit specific instruction at the time of their occurrence.

Units of instruction can comprise one or more program objectives. As the term is used here, unit refers simply to an indication of program objectives, logically grouped for instruction, which specify the order of teaching and the amount of time allotted to instruction on each program objective within the unit.

The arrangement of logical clusters of program objectives into effective teaching units is largely a creative act of competent teachers. The almost infinite amount of combinations of program objectives makes it difficult to cover all possibilities. The key criteria by which to judge teacher competence in this area are: "Was the unit effective?" "Did its implementation result in a significant number of students making meaningful gains in performance on the objectives of the unit?" Another key criterion is, "Can the unit be sufficiently described so that it could be implemented again a year or two later by another teacher or in another school with similar students?" This latter criterion, the ability to describe instructional procedures sufficiently well so that they can be replicated without being overly prescriptive, is the focus of Chapters 7 and 8.

Chapter 7

Designing Effective Instruction

As suggested in Chapter 6, it is important to design instruction in a way that meets several criteria. These include:

1. Instruction that is clearly linked to the objectives of the program
2. Instructional materials and procedures that are consistent with the research on effective instruction
3. Instructional materials are organized in a way that facilitates flexibility of teacher use, while maintaining the ability to be replicated.

The refusal of many physical educators to clearly identify the objectives of their instruction has led to the use of diffuse methods and procedures, which in turn has contributed to modest and scattered effects, most of which have gone undocumented. Specification of the intents of instruction in terms of goals and objectives is necessary for the three phases of effective instruction: planning, implementation, and evaluation. The importance of goals and objectives to planning has been addressed in previous chapters and their importance to evaluation will be addressed in subsequent chapters. This chapter will emphasize the importance of effective instruction on student outcomes.

Physical educators must reject the notion that teaching many good activities will translate into defensible programs or that the benefits of activity to the quality of life will automatically occur. There is overwhelming evidence that the practice of exposing students to physical activities and hoping for positive results in unspecified outcomes persists. The knowledge, skill, fitness capacities, attitudes, and practices of the adult population as well as those of recent graduates are testimony to the futility of this method. We must reverse the instructional approach from teaching activities that may contribute to objectives to one of identifying high-priority objectives and selecting activities to help students attain them.

DESIGN OF EFFECTIVE INSTRUCTION

Using a Model to Guide Instruction

Effective instruction is the foundation of exemplary programs. The degree to which students achieve the objectives of the program is directly related to the quality of instruction that they receive during class and extra-class periods devoted to practice or training. Some of the characteristics of outstanding instruction and programs are:

- Clear communication of "what" is to be learned (objectives which represent knowledge, skills, fitness capacities, and/or personal-social skills)
- Evaluation of students' abilities relative to the objectives of the instruction
- Use of a systematic model of instruction that incorporates guidelines for effective instruction
- Evaluation of student progress and alteration of instruction in accordance with the degree to which the objectives have been achieved.

Clear Communication of the Content to be Learned: Students will not achieve instructional objectives merely through exposure and practice; they must have specific feedback revealing what they are doing correctly and, equally as important, what they are doing incorrectly. Specific feedback cannot be clearly communicated without clear identification of the objective to be learned and the key elements of its performance. By focusing on the instructional objectives and their key elements, instructors can clearly communicate to students what they are requested to learn. This procedure alone is often enough to dramatically improve students' achievement.

Evaluation of Students' Abilities: It is important to evaluate students' abilities on the objectives incorporated in the program to determine their instructional needs. The relationship between instructional objectives, students' performance levels, and instruction is illustrated in Chapter 5, Figure 5-3. Evaluation of students' status is necessary to provide specific feedback to the students relative to portions of the objective they have attained and what is left to accomplish. Without such evaluation and feedback, instruction will be less effective.

A Model for Instruction: Although there are many ways to design instruction, the following approach has proven to be both easy to use and effective in teaching and/or refining skills.

1. Get the attention of the students.
2. Communicate precisely what needs to be learned.
3. Provide for practice and feedback.
4. Evaluate results and take appropriate action.

Each portion of this approach is briefly addressed in the following paragraphs.

Get the attention of the students: The attention of the students must be directed at the instructor before instruction can be effective. Establish the precedent that when you speak, important information is being communicated. Conveying to students the need for competence on the skill or ability is one way to gain their attention. An example of how a local, regional, or national level performer has mastered the skill and has used it to great advantage is often a good way to elicit interest. Communicating to students that they need instruction on the skill is also helpful. Some instructors accomplish this with the following steps:

1. Briefly describe the new skill and then let the students try it several times in a quick-paced drill setting.

2. Carefully observe their performance and identify their strengths and weaknesses. (Use the key elements of the skill as a basis for your observations.)

3. Call them back and report your observations to them in a group, prior to additional instruction.

This approach provides a believable base from which common weaknesses in performance on one or more key elements can be described. This type of an approach will enhance the instructor's credibility and will help motivate the students to listen to instruction. Also, subsequent teaching can be specifically matched to the needs (weaknesses) that were observed. If students have already achieved the desired skill level, then instruction can be shifted to another program objective.

Communicate precisely what needs to be learned: When instructors and students know their status on a given instructional objective, conditions are well established for teaching and learning. Individuals learn most efficiently when they focus on one aspect of a skill at a time. Demonstrations and verbal descriptions help the students know exactly how they are progressing in relation to the objective that they are trying to achieve.

Provide for practice and feedback: Organize the lesson and select the teaching-learning activities, drills, games, or practice activities to provide students with the following types of support.

1. As many repetitions (trials) as possible within the allotted time for instruction.

2. Specific, immediate, and positive feedback on what they did correctly and what they can do to improve.

3. Encouragement to try again.

Repetitions and feedback are essential to learning. There will be a direct relationship between gains in student performance and the degree to which these two dimensions of instruction occur.

Feedback can be dramatically increased by using student peers as instructional aids. Where instruction is focused on clearly stated key elements of performance and the important aspects of performing the skill have been effectively communicated, students are often as good (and sometimes better) at seeing discrepancies in a partner's performance as are adults. Working in pairs or small groups can thus be very effective in increasing both the number of trials and the amount of feedback that individuals get within a given amount of practice time. Also, by providing feedback, students will improve their understanding of the performance requirements of the objective.

Evaluate results and take appropriate action: Evaluations of student performance must occur on a continuing basis during instruction. This is the only way to answer the question, "Are the students achieving the objectives?" If the students are making progress, enjoy it. The instructional process is working. Perhaps, however, it can be made more efficient. Are there ways that the same results can be obtained in less time? Can even greater gains be achieved within the same time allotment?

If students are not achieving the instructional objectives, it is important to ask, "Why?" Although it is possible that a number of students are inept at learning, this is seldom the case. First, assume that the results are related to inappropriate instruction or insufficient instructional time. A good approach to answering the question "Why?" is to reconsider the planning, teaching, communicating, discipline, or other instructional inputs that may have influenced the results, and attempt to determine what could be improved. Subsequent lessons can then be altered accordingly. Continuous trial, error, and revisions will result in improved effectiveness, which ultimately translates into increased student achievement.

The design of effective instruction is facilitated by considering materials, methods, and procedures that fit within a model of instruction. Some of the methods and/or procedures are briefly described in the preceding paragraphs. The section that follows on guidelines for effective instruction is written to assist teachers with the design and conduct of effective instruction.

GUIDELINES FOR EFFECTIVE INSTRUCTION

As teachers develop lessons to maximize the practice and feedback opportunities for their students, they should use guidelines for effective instruction that have been revealed by recent research. Several guidelines are presented below, followed by brief descriptions of their meanings and how they can be used.

1. Set realistic expectations
2. Structure instruction
3. Establish an orderly environment
4. Group your students according to ability
5. Maximize on-task time
6. Maximize the success rate
7. Monitor progress
8. Ask questions
9. Promote a sense of control

Set Realistic Expectations

The expectations teachers communicate to their students can create a positive climate for learning that will influence the achievement of their students (Rutter, Maugham, Mortmore & Ousten, 1979). Clear and attainable goals for performance and expenditure of effort will facilitate achievement. A recent review (Fisher, Berliner, Filby, Marliave, Cahen & Dishaw, 1980) listed the reasons associated with this occurrence.

> In comparison to students for whom teachers hold high expectations about performance, the students perceived to be low performers are more often positioned farther away from the teacher; treated as groups, not individuals; smiled at less; made eye contact with less; called on less to answer questions; are given less time to answer questions; have their answers responded to less frequently; are praised more often for marginal and inadequate responses; are praised less frequently for successful responses; and are interrupted more often.

Teachers and former students will be able to understand how even a few of the above actions could reduce motivation and achievement. What is saddening is that many capable children are inappropriately labeled as non-achievers on the basis of delayed maturity, poor experience, body size, body composition, and/or many other factors that mask their true abilities. Yet, if expectations are low, achievement will also decrease. There are at least two important messages in this guideline:

- Expect that, as the instructor, you are going to significantly improve the skills, knowledge of rules and strategies, and attitudes of every one of your students during the course of instruction.

- Set realistic goals for your students. Make a commitment to help each student achieve the next level of performance in the achievement progression and expect that improvement to occur.

Structure Instruction

Student achievement has been strongly linked to: 1) clear communication of intended outcomes (objectives of instruction), 2) explanations of why the goals and objectives are important (essential or prerequisite skills), and 3) descriptions of what to do to achieve outcomes (instructional directions) (Bruner, 1981; Fisher *et al.*, 1980). Effective instruction is based upon the systematic organization of the content to be taught. The critical steps to take are as follows.

1. Select the essential program objectives from the many options available.

2. Clearly identify the elements of acceptable performance for each objective included in the lesson.

3. Organize and conduct instruction to maximize the opportunities students have to acquire the objectives by using the effective teaching practices contained in this chapter

Establish an Orderly Environment

Student achievement is related to the following elements (Fisher, Filby, Marliave, Cahen, Dishaw, Moore & Berliner, 1978):

- an orderly, safe, businesslike environment with clear expectations;
- student accountability for effort and achievement; and
- rewards for achievement of expectations.

A note of caution is in order. Strong, over-controlled implementation of these findings can cause frustration and anxiety, but under-control can lead to lack of achievement. The best of circumstances is a relaxed, enjoyable, but businesslike environment. The ability to balance these two opposing forces to maximize achievement and enjoyment by keeping both in perspective may be one of the most difficult tasks teachers face.

Group the Students

Decisions about the size and composition of groups for various learning tasks are complex, and they are related to achievement (Webb, 1980). Typically in groups of mixed abilities, the child with average ability suffers a loss in achievement, while the child with low ability does slightly better. The critical condition for grouping to be effective is to have students practicing at the skill levels needed to advance their performance abilities. Although this can be difficult to achieve, most effective teachers design practices that maximize this principle of individualized instruction.

Physical education classes will always have individuals at many different levels of ability on the objectives included in the program. This situation presents a seemingly impossible grouping task. There are, however, some good solutions to this problem.

- When a new skill or cognitive concept is being taught that all of the students need to know, use a single group instructional setting.
- As differences in ability are identified, seek to place students of similar ability in smaller groups.
- When a skill or cognitive concept is being practiced by students at several levels of ability (initial, intermediate, or advanced), establish learning stations in which each group of students is asked to focus on achievement of the next levels.

Designing Effective Instruction

The placement of students into groups for learning the skills, cognitive concepts, or other capacities must be independently decided for each objective. A student placed at a high level on one program objective will not necessarily remain at a high level on another program objective. It is important that the following conditions be established for every group of students.

1. Order must be established and maintained at each learning station. (An assistant may be necessary.)
2. Task(s) that are to be mastered at each station must be clearly communicated to the students.
3. Many trial opportunities must be provided.
4. A means for giving immediate, specific, and positive feedback must be established.

Maximize On-task Time

Reports of research that document the amount of time that students are active in the learning process (rather than standing in lines or watching others perform) reveal that actual "engaged" learning time in practices is regularly less than 50 percent, and often falls to five to 10 percent of the total time available for practice. Instruction that wastes an already limited amount of instructional time is neither effective nor efficient. As an instructor, there are several actions that can be taken to maximize the use of available time.

1. Reduce the number of students who are waiting in line by using more sub-groups in drills.
2. Provide sufficient amounts of equipment so that students do not have to wait for practice attempts.
3. Reduce the transition time between drills by preplanning lessons to minimize the reformulation of groups and establishment of new equipment configurations.
4. Use instructional grouping practices that have students practicing skills at their appropriate performance level.
5. Use aids (paid, parents, older students or peers) to assist with the instruction at each station.

Remember: saving five minutes a day across 36 weeks of two lessons per week equals 360 minutes of instructional time for each student. Time gained by effective organization becomes available for teaching and practicing other program objectives.

Maximize the Success Rate

The relationship between successful experiences, achievement, and motivation to learn is very strong (Fisher *et al.*, 1978; Rosenshine, 1983). The basic message in this research is to ask students to attempt new learnings that will yield 70 percent to 90 percent successful experiences. This level of success will motivate them to want to continue to achieve. There are two major implications for effective teaching.

- Reduce each program and instructional objective to achievable sub-skills and focus instruction on those sub-skills (see the developmental progressions suggested in Chapter 8).
- Provide feedback to the students such that, on most occasions, something that they did is rewarded, followed by specific instructions about what needs more work, ending with an encouraging, "try again."

Monitor Progress

If lessons are organized to allow students to work at several stations in accordance with their current abilities and needs, it follows that students often will be working independently or in small groups. When students are left to work on their own, they often spend less time engaged in the activities for which they are responsible. When teachers are actively moving about, monitoring progress, and providing individual and small group instructional feedback, students will make greater gains (Fisher et al., 1978). Within this context teachers can provide much corrective feedback, contingent praise, and emotionally neutral criticism (not personal attacks or sarcasm) for inappropriate behavior. These actions have a positive influence on both achievement and attitude.

Ask Questions

Asking questions also relates to student achievement (Brophy, J. E. & Evertson, C., 1976). Questions should promote participation and establish, reinforce, and/or reveal factual data associated with a skill, rule, capacity, strategy, or attitude. Use of this teaching technique seems to work best when there is a pause of three or more seconds before asking for a response. During this time students should be cued to think about the answer (Rowe, 1974).

Promote a Sense of Control

Students should feel that they have some control over their destiny to achieve mastery of the program objectives. A sense of control can be developed several ways.

- Organizing instruction to result in many successful experiences (*i.e.*, opportunities to provide positive feedback).
- Teaching students that individuals learn skills at different rates and to use effort and their own continuous progress on an objective as their primary guide to determining achievement.

- Encouraging individual students to put forth their best efforts. Reward such effort with a comment, pat on the back, thumbs up sign, or other means.

In these ways, students learn that the harder they work and the more they try, the greater their gains will be. At the same time you will be reducing the natural feeling of inferiority or inability that grows in the presence of feedback that is limited to pointing out errors. Although some students will work toward objectives in almost any practice situation, many potentially excellent students will not continue when they feel there is no possibility of gaining your approval.

The information in this chapter provides a base from which effective instructional resource materials and instruction can be developed. Objective-related instructional resource materials, written in accordance with the literature on effective instruction, provide teachers with the information necessary to develop strong lessons without prescribing that they teach lesson one on day one, lesson two on day two, and so on. As will be discussed in Chapter 8, the need in physical education for objective-related instruction resource materials is critical to the development of exemplary programs.

Chapter 8

Developing Resource Materials

THE NEED FOR RESOURCE MATERIALS

The phrase "exemplary physical education program" describes a program that is effective and that contains procedures and materials that may be helpful to other individuals who seek to develop effective programs. However, a program that has demonstrated significant outcomes in students' achievements but is not sufficiently described to be repeatable falls short of the expectations associated with the term "exemplary." Prior to the time that an effective program, instructional event, or procedure can be shared with others, it must be described in sufficient detail so that others may adopt it or extract its salient parts for replication.

The essential characteristic of repeatability mandates that instructional resource materials be available as a record of how the content was taught. The context within which the instruction occurred must also be on record. When instructional materials are written, taught, modified, and rewritten to reflect the changes made during implementation, they serve as the final record of what was taught, how it was taught, how the students responded to the instructional content and procedures, and how effective the lessons were in changing students' competence.

Providing effective resource materials gives teachers information from which the instruction can be designed (and maintains) sufficient flexibility for them to retain their creativity in planning and teaching the lessons. The use of resource materials is recommended in lieu of providing a series of packaged lessons, which tend to stifle the involvement of teachers in the planning of appropriate instruction.

Having printed resource materials that relate to the objectives to be achieved also has the advantage that the resource materials may be constantly improved as teachers find more effective ways to accomplish their objectives. As additional information about the skills, knowledge, fitness, or affective levels of the students becomes available, it can be incorporated into the existing resource materials and used by all teachers.

Perhaps the most important reason for having a dynamic reservoir of resource materials is that it provides an opportunity for experienced teachers to share their years of accumulated wisdom. If experienced teachers and those just entering teaching both contribute to and draw from this reservoir, the reservoir will grow to become a valuable concentration of instructional

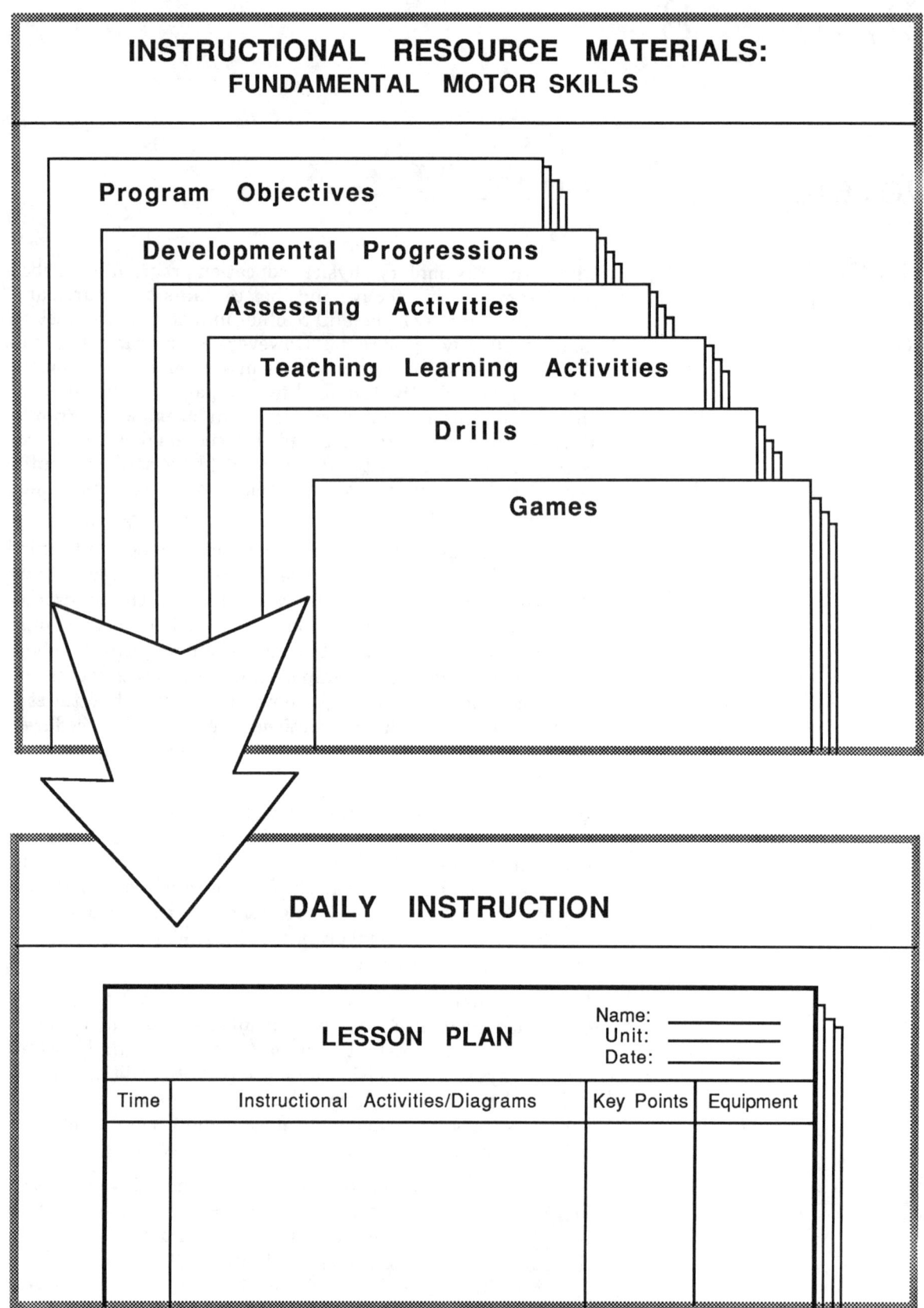

Figure 8.1. Relationship between instructional resource materials and daily lessons

INSTRUCTIONAL RESOURCE MATERIALS

resource materials. Failing to maintain a written account of the materials and procedures used by experienced teachers results in the loss of important information when teachers retire, change jobs, or leave the school systems.

Materials that are essential to good instruction must eventually be incorporated into a daily plan of instruction, commonly called a lesson plan. However, the lesson plans of teachers in programs that are exemplary must reflect the scope and sequence of the entire curriculum as it relates to the specific content of the unit with which they are currently involved. Rather than representing an arbitrary selection of content that the teacher would enjoy teaching on a specific day, the lesson plan should contain the accumulated wisdom of all the teachers in the district who have had the responsibility of achieving the specific objectives of a particular grade level.

This rather idealistic description of what each lesson plan must accomplish implies that it must be constructed with care from materials that relate to the overall physical education program. Lesson planning that fits this description can only be developed if the resource materials that contribute the substance to the plans contain the 1) program objectives; 2) developmental progressions of the skills, fitness capacities, values, and knowledge; 3) activities to be used in assessing students' status and progress; and 4) teaching-learning activities, including drills and games. The relationship between instructional resource materials and the lessons of daily instruction is illustrated in Figure 8-1 and will be discussed briefly in the subsequent subsections.

PROGRAM OBJECTIVE: OVERHAND THROW

Instructional Objective 1

Demonstrate appropriate throwing form two consecutive times

　　a. Side orientation to initiate the throw
　　b. Weight transfer to the foot opposite the throwing arm as the throwing arm passes the shoulder
　　c. Hip, followed by shoulder rotation during the throwing motion
　　d. Arm action initiated with a near complete downward extension of the arm (hand on top of the ball)
　　e. Hand passes above and outside of the shoulder

Instructional Objective 2

Maintain appropriate throwing form and hit a six-foot-square target placed one foot above the ground from a distance of 40 feet, two consecutive times

---

Figure 8.2. Example program and instructional objective

Program Objectives

The definition and development of program objectives was discussed in Chapter 5. The illustration in Figure 8-2 depicts how program objectives for the skill of overhand throwing may be further reduced to sub-objectives, more commonly referred to as **instructional objectives and their key elements**. When expressed in this fashion, the intents of instruction can be clearly communicated to instructors, students, and interested others.

Developmental Progressions

Teachers are aware that learners can only relate positively to challenges that are within their realm of comprehension and attainment. For this reason, teachers must know the students' various abilities to respond to specific requests for their best efforts, whether the objective is skill development, affective behavior, physical fitness, or cognitive function. This range of responses has been called levels, stages, and hierarchies, but we have used the term **developmental progressions** to describe the sequence of events, from rudimentary to mature or simple to complex, which characterize the responses of students to a specific objective. An example of a **developmental progression** for learning the skill of overhand throwing is provided in Figure 8-3. Blank forms, suitable for reproduction are included in Appendix I, Example Instructional Materials and Forms.

Assessing Activity

Each instructional activity must be accompanied by one or more ways to determine the initial capabilities of students in relation to the objective, and subsequently, to determine if any progress has been made toward achieving the objective. These ways of determining status or progress are called **assessing activities.** They may exist in the form of written tests, observational, behavioral checklists, or activities for students that provide a context conducive to assessing student status on one or more objectives. Whatever their form, teachers should describe assessing activities with sufficient clarity that others could read the descriptions and transfer the information to practice in a teaching-learning setting. An example form for recording activities is illustrated in Figure 8-4. Appendix I includes an example assessing activity for the program objective, "overhand throw," and reproducible blanks for writing other assessing activities.

Teaching-learning Activity

The various means that teachers use to facilitate the acquisition of instructional objectives is described under the phrase **teaching-learning activity**. It includes an indication of how much time will be spent on each phase of the instruction, a diagram and instructions for each activity, the key points to be emphasized as each activity is presented, and the equipment that may be needed for teaching each activity. Figure 8-5 contains an example form for recording teaching-learning activities, and Appendix I provides an example for the program objective, "overhand throw." Note that the lower portion of the form contains a space for the teacher to report useful information about how the situation could be altered in subsequent sessions.

Drills

Improving the performance of students is directly related to the time they spend under appropriate guidance in attempting to achieve a specific objective. This phenomenon, commonly called "time-on-task," is most efficiently accomplished through the use of activities called **drills**, which are organized so that students receive a maximum number of trials on a specific objective in a limited amount of time. Repetition of performance designed to elicit the next higher level of behavior is the primary criterion for a good drill. Figure 8-6 contains a form for recording drills, and Appendix I includes an example drill that is designed to provide a context for improving performance in the overhand throw.

Games

One of the overriding goals of any physical education program is to provide its students with sufficient competence so that they are able to translate what they have learned into their lifestyles as adults. The category of resource materials titled **games** is an example of how many separate skills may be combined into a common form of activity wherein the objective may encompass skill development, leisure, fitness, enjoyment, social development, or any combination of objectives. The primary purpose of **games**, as they are used in this guide to exemplary physical education programs, is to incorporate one skill or a series of skills, rules, and strategies into a more complex situation as is frequently required of individuals in the games and sports of our society. Figure 8-7 contains a form for recording the rules, strategies, instructional activities, key points, and equipment needed for games, and Appendix I provides an example game that incorporates the skill of overhand throwing into the playing of a game related to softball.

The numerous components of a good lesson plan are shown in Figure 8-8. Note that the three parts of the lesson incorporate the elements that were discussed in the subsection Guidelines for Effective Instruction in Chapter 7. In addition, the lesson template is intended to be used as a guide for instructional planning by drawing from prepared resource materials to create an effective teaching episode.

SUMMARY

An exemplary program of physical education must be supported by a comprehensive reservoir of resource materials that pertain to the program's instructional objectives. For efficiency, these resource materials should be arranged by program and instructional objectives and include developmental progressions, assessing activities, teaching-learning activities, games, and drills. The purpose of the resource materials is twofold.

1. To provide access, by teachers, to the legacy of effective instructional techniques, organizational patterns, drills, and games that have been developed through the experience of veteran teachers.

2. To infuse the materials that have proven to be effective into the curriculum in conjunction with new information that may not currently be a part of the instructional techniques of experienced teachers.

The instructional resource materials are viewed as being in a constant state of development. As better, more efficient, methods and content become available, they are incorporated into the existing materials and tested by other teachers. Eventually, the achievements of students will indicate which teachers are most successful in manipulating a variety of variables as they strive for the desired outcomes, but maintaining and promoting resource materials is one of the most cost-effective ways to enhance effective instruction and the professional development of teachers.

Developing Resource Materials 51

DEVELOPMENTAL PROGRESSIONS

Program Objective: _Overhand throw_   Name: _Smith_   Date: _12-3-86_

STEP	TASK	GRADE*
1	Throw a tennis sized ball with the combined action of the hand, arm and shoulder	
2	Throw a tennis ball with at least one of the following key elements a. Side orientation to initiate the throw b. Weight transfer to the foot opposite the throwing arm as the throwing arm passes the shoulder c. Hip, followed by shoulder, rotation during the throwing motion d. Arm action initiated with a near complete downward extension of the arm (hand on top of the ball) e. Hand passes above and outside of the shoulder	
3	Throw a tennis ball with at least 2 of the above elements of mature form	
4	Throw a tennis ball with at least 3 of the above elements of mature form	
5	Throw a tennis ball with at least 4 of the above elements of mature form	

*Grade level where teachers can expect that 80% of the children will be able to adequately perform the task.

Figure 8.3. Example of a developmental progression for throwing

DEVELOPMENTAL PROGRESSIONS

Program Objective: Overhand throw (cont.)

Name: _____
Date: _____

STEP	TASK	GRADE*
6	Throw a tennis ball with all 5 of the above elements of mature form	
7**	Throw a tennis ball at least 30' with all of the above elements of mature form, 2 consecutive times	
8	Throw a ball at least 40' with mature form	
9	Throw a ball 30' and hit an 8' square target while maintaining mature form	
10	Throw a ball 30' and hit a six foot square target while maintaining mature form 2 consecutive times	
11**	Throw a ball 40' and hit a six ft. square target while maintaining mature form, 2 consecutive times	

**Exactly equal to Instructional Objective #1 and #2.

*Grade level where teachers can expect that 80% of the children will be able to adequately perform the task.

Figure 8.3. (cont.) Example of a developmental progression for throwing

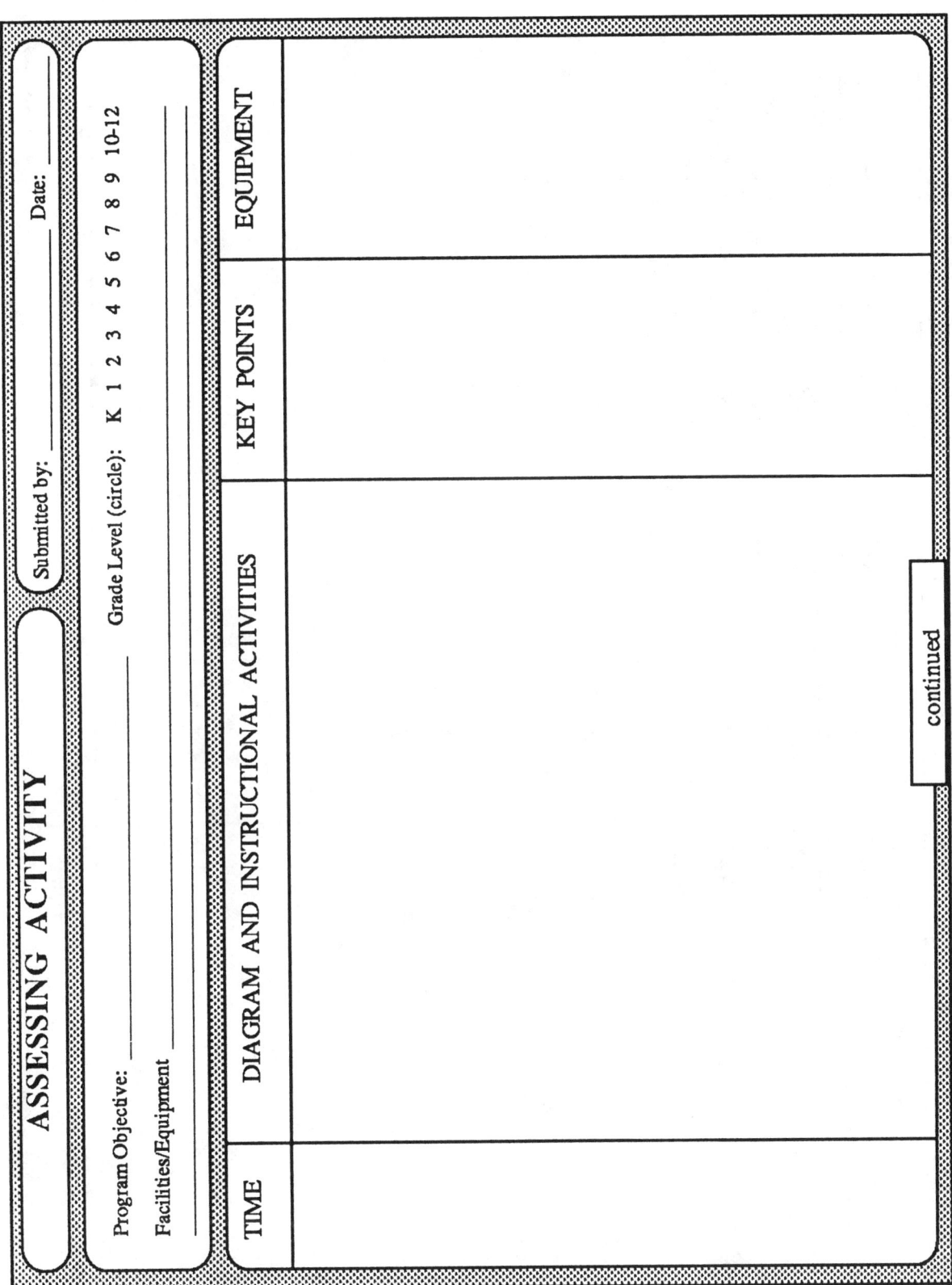

Figure 8.4. Example form for recording assessing activities

TIME	DIAGRAM AND INSTRUCTIONAL ACTIVITIES	KEY POINTS	EQUIPMENT

NOTES, VARIATIONS, HELPFUL COMMENTS

Figure 8.4., page 2

Developing Resource Materials

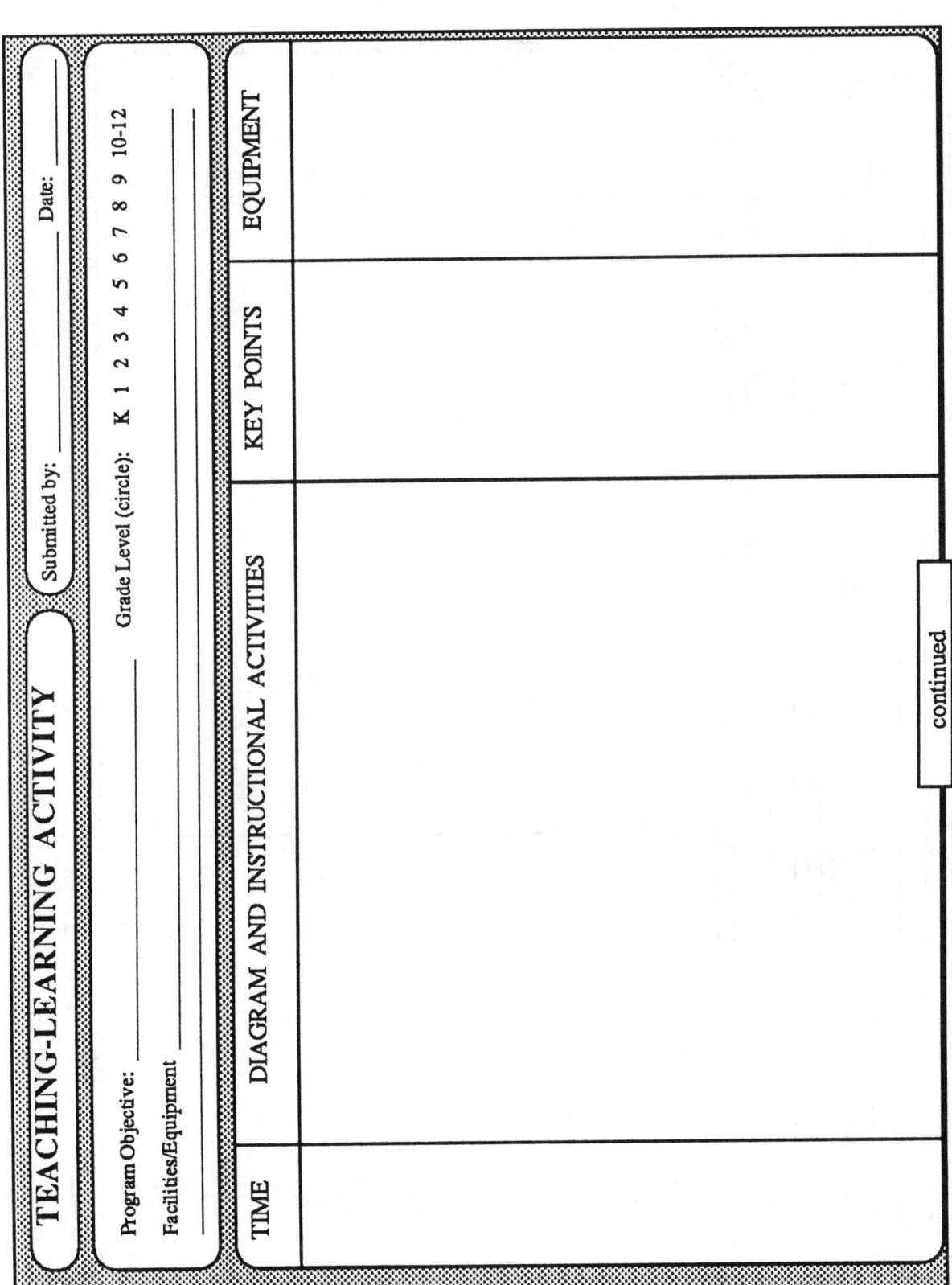

Figure 8.5. Example form for recording teaching-learning activities

TIME	DIAGRAM AND INSTRUCTIONAL ACTIVITIES	KEY POINTS	EQUIPMENT

NOTES, VARIATIONS, HELPFUL COMMENTS

Figure 8.5., page 2

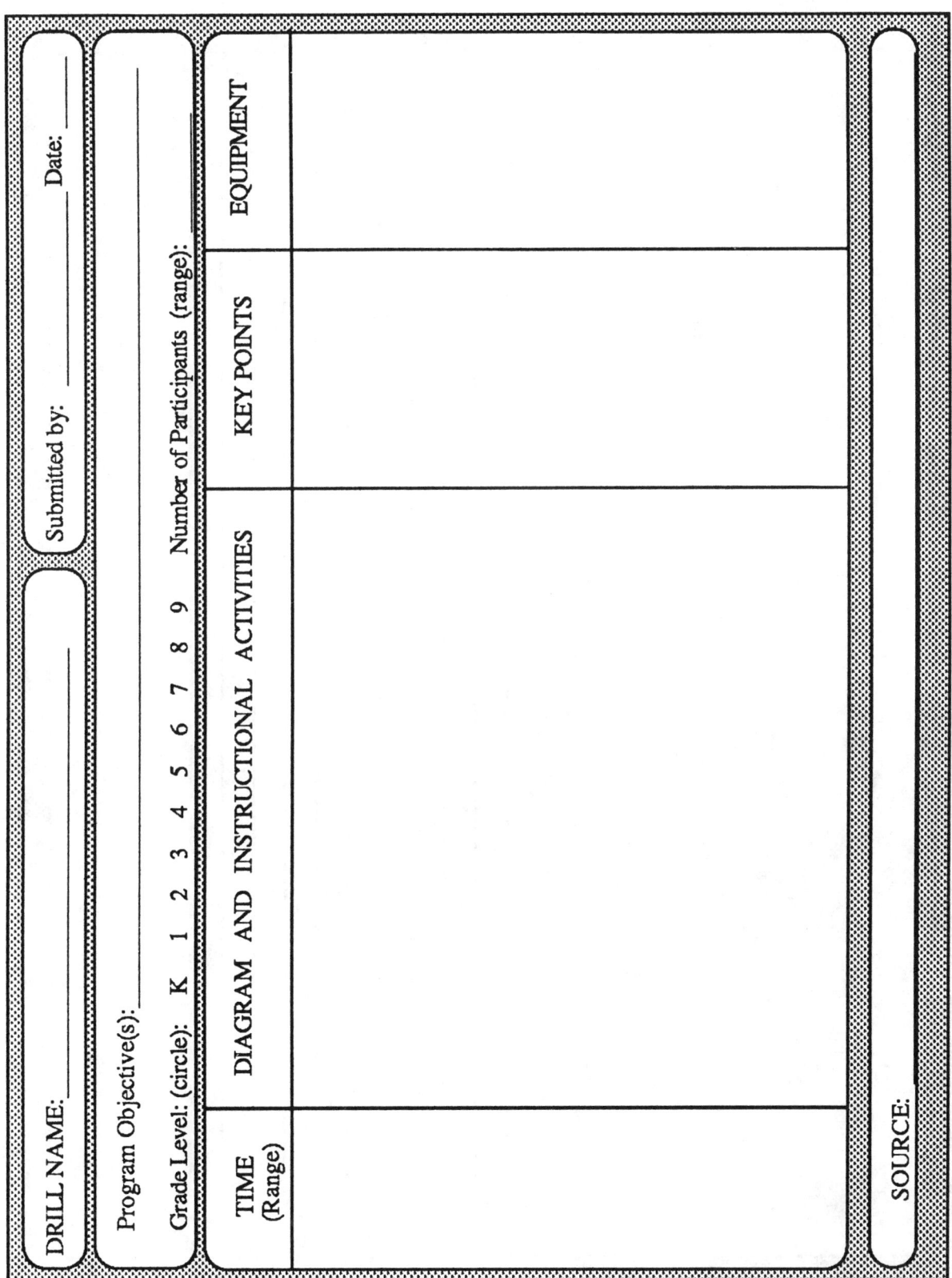

Figure 8.6. Example form for recording skills

NOTES / VARIATIONS / HELPFUL COMMENTS:

Figure 8.6., page 2

Developing Resource Materials 59

GAME NAME: _____ Submitted by: _____ Date: _____

Program Objective(s): _____

Grade Level (circle): K 1 2 3 4 5 6 7 8 9 10-12   Number of Players (Range): _____

Facilities/Equipment _____

Rules of Play (Object of the Game, Rules, Fouls, Penalties, Scoring): _____

SOURCE: _____

Figure 8.7. Example form for recording games

TIME (Range)	DIAGRAM AND INSTRUCTIONAL ACTIVITIES	KEY POINTS	EQUIPMENT

NOTES:

Figure 8.7., page 2

Introductory Activities [1]

1. Gain attention and/or motivate (to achieve the objective).
    Arouse interest, establish purpose for achieving the objective, get the body's sensors ready. Unusual, eye catching, and/or creative.
2. Review prerequisite skills needed.
3. State the objective(s) of the instruction.
4. Set the perspective.
    How does this objective relate to past and/or future objectives, work, and/or game applications?

Instruction [2]

5. Review the skill, knowledge, or capacity to be taught.
    Briefly explain the objective and its key component(s) and demonstrate or illustrate the desired outcome.
6. Engage the students in a trial of the objective. Assess their strengths and weaknesses. [3]
7. Focus student learning (teach) on appropriate key component.
    Group as appropriate (by key component of the objective, instructional objective level, or step in the developmental progression of the objective).
8. Repeat (seven above) with the next key component.

Summarize [1]

9. Provide closure and set up the next lesson.
    Summarize key points, ask (and answer) pertinent questions, explain how this objective(s) can transfer to other similar (or dissimilar) objectives, indicate practice and/or self test activities that will help acquire the objective or key component, or relate how this objective fits into the student evaluation procedures.

---

1. Warm up or cool down as appropriate
2. See guidelines for effective instruction
3. Record status or changes in performance as appropriate

Figure 8.8. Components of a lesson plan

Chapter 9

Evaluation of Student Status and Progress

Completing the decisions of what to teach and when (Chapters 3 to 6), provides direction for the entire educational effort. Program goals and their corresponding objectives, clearly stated as the intended focus of the instructional process, provide the basis for appropriate student evaluation. The goals, program, and instruction represent what the staff and the community desire their students to learn. Student evaluation, then, is the process of determining and reporting the degree to which these intended results have occurred.

There are at least four reasons for evaluating student status and progress:

1. Frequent evaluation of student progress facilitates appropriate prescriptive changes in day-to-day teaching.

2. Evaluation of student achievement of stated objectives facilitates reporting progress to students, parents, and administrators.

3. The effects of instruction, summarized across students, provides an important base of information for identifying strengths and weaknesses of the program.

4. The achievements of students, when compared to program objectives, provides the basis for program improvements.

Student evaluation is the base from which evaluation of program effectiveness is determined. Evaluation of program effectiveness, however, requires establishing more rigorous procedures in the control of instruction, measurement of achievements, and analysis of the data in order to produce believable results. The evaluation of program effectiveness will be discussed in Chapter 10.

KEY FEATURES OF STUDENT EVALUATION

Student Status and Progress

As indicated in Chapter 5, the assessment of student status and progress must be relative to some standard. In an objectives-related program, the primary comparative standards are the stated program and instructional objectives. Student status is determined, therefore, in relation to mastery or non-mastery of the instructional objectives or their component parts. The relationship between instructional objectives and student performance is illustrated in Figure 9-1. Using this illustration, a student who enters an instructional episode without the elements of the form described by Instructional Objective 1 (appropriate form) and subsequently obtains the elements of appropriate form as a result of instruction, would have made a defined gain in performance status. Thus, measuring student status at two points in time provides estimates of student progress.

Objective-Related Student Evaluation

Program Objective: To demonstrate competence on the overhand throw

Instructional Objective	Corresponding Student Performance Levels

1. Appropriate form, *i.e.*:
  a. weight transfer
  b. arm action
  c. rotation
  d. etc.
	1. Inappropriate form
	
	2. Appropriate form

2. Appropriate form plus functional ability, *i.e.*, form plus:
  a. distance
  b. accuracy
	3. Form plus function

Note that the performance criteria of Instructional Objective 1 divides students into two categories [*i.e.*, those with inappropriate form (✓-) and those with appropriate form (✓). Similarly, Instructional Objective 2 further divides students into those that have achieved the form performance criteria of Instructional Objective 1 (✓) and those who have achieved distance and/or accuracy criteria (✓+)]

Figure 9.1. Relationship between instructional objectives and the evaluation of student performance

Status and Progress Relative to Peers

Parents are most frequently interested in student status relative to some desirable standard. Typically, they are also interested in improvement. The third bit of information that parents desire is how their child is doing relative to other children of a similar age and gender. This information is often communicated to parents in terms of their child's performance status relative to the rest of the class. In this approach, the standard for comparison is relative to the class (a norm-referenced model) rather than relative to the stated objective (a mastery model). Both approaches are illustrated in Figure 9-2.

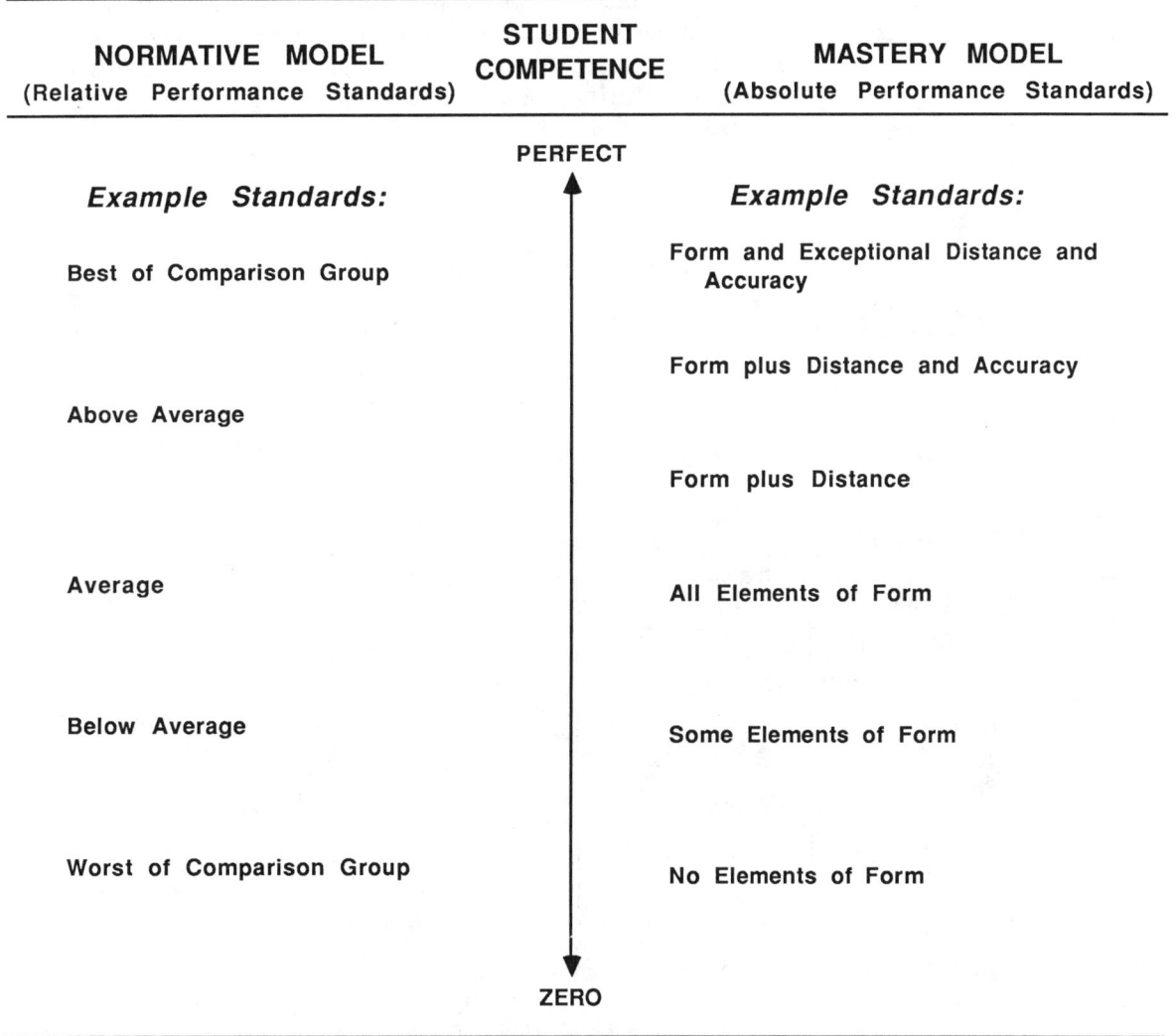

Figure 9.2. Characteristics of two models for describing student performance

When the norm group is large (several classes or more), this model may provide a good standard for comparing students' status relative to their peers. It is always possible, however, to be the best in the group and still not have achieved a desirable level of mastery. This is particularly true where the normative standards have been acquired from an unfit or poorly instructed comparison group. Accordingly, the best approach to use when describing an individual's performance relative to peers is to indicate the percent of his or her peers who have attained similar student performance levels on the criterion involving mastery of the instructional objective.

Feasibility

Procedures for evaluating students' achievements must be feasible. Accordingly, the evaluation of students' achievement will be more informal than that which is acceptable as evidence for documenting program effectiveness. The differences between evaluation of students' performance for the purposes of refining instruction, reporting status, and progress versus demonstrating evidence of program effectiveness are illustrated in Figure 9-3.

Student Evaluation:
Levels of Measurement Formality

Evaluation Types	Evaluation Purpose	Formality	Participants
Evaluation for Instruction	To determine student status on instructional objectives (or steps of the developmental progressions	Informal (expedient, feasible)	All Students
Evaluation for Program Effectiveness		Formal (reliable, valid)	Representative Samples of Students

Figure 9.3. Differences in formality of student evaluation

As illustrated in Figure 9-1, division of each program objective into two instructional objectives provides three levels of student performance. These three divisions can be represented by the symbols ✓-, ✓ or ✓+, indicators of status commonly used by physical educators to represent student performance. Using these or other symbols in combination with a record page in the grade book or a separate sheet of paper similar to that illustrated in Figure 9-4 and included as a reproducible blank format in Appendix J provides an informal means of monitoring student status and progress.

Evaluation of Student Status and Progress

Student Performance Score Sheet

Instructor: _____
Class: _____
Year: _____
Unit: _____

SCORING

1 = incomplete form
2 = form
3 = form + function

Unit Objectives

Name

Totals

TOTALS

Figure 9.4. Example student performance score sheet

Reassessment conducted only at the end of an instructional unit is unattractive because it has no prescriptive utility. Much of the benefit of providing feedback to students is lost when this information cannot be used to enhance performance. The most desirable frequency for obtaining data on students' performance is on a lesson-to-lesson basis. Changes in behavior should be noted and recorded at any time in the instructional process that students achieve the next level of performance.

Data on students' performance may be obtained at stations through self and peer evaluation; accompanied with verification by teacher observation within instruction, game, or drill activities; or gathered through formal evaluation sessions. Less formal assessments are typically more feasible in terms of use of instructional time. Efficient use of these evaluation techniques will allow creative instructors to evaluate students' status and progress within the 10 to 15 percent of total instructional time available in a way that provides credibility to the staff, program, and school district.

Reporting Student Progress

Meaningful reports to students, parents, and others are extremely important if the program is to maintain its credibility. Complete reports should include at least the following information.

1. The content (objectives) that has been taught
2. The student's entry and exit status relative to the objectives
3. The amount of change that has occurred
4. An indication of the student's status relative that of his/her peers

Content

The foundation upon which the reporting of students' achievement should be based is the program objectives that form the instructional program. Accordingly, a report of student progress should be based upon the degree to which that content has been mastered. As simple and logical as the relationship between objectives and outcomes may seem, the evaluation of student performance in physical education has infrequently been related to the achievement of stated objectives. Student evaluations (when conducted) are typically based upon some standardized test of motor performance, motor development, fitness, and/or selected sport skills. To the extent that these tests match the objectives included in the program, they may yield appropriate information. Most often, however, the tests are not selected with due consideration for their match with the program objectives. Consequently, they measure only a small portion of the total instructional program. Evaluations of this type, therefore, are unacceptable for identifying and reporting student gains.

STUDENT PERFORMANCE PROFILE

Name: _____ Date: _____

School: _____ Grade: _____

GOALS / OBJECTIVES	Performance Level			Change	%ile Age/Gender		
	1	2	3		1	2	3
FUNDAMENTAL MOTOR SKILLS							
Run	X						
Jump	X						
Hop	X						
Skip	X						
O. Throw		X					
Catch			X				
Strike	X						
U. Roll			X				
etc.							
PHYSICAL FITNESS							
Aerobic capacity	X						
Arm-shoulder strength E.	X						
Abdominal strength E.		X					
Leg strength E.							
Hip-trunk flexibility	X		X				
Arm-shoulder flexibility		X					
% body fat	X						
COGNITIVE							
Beneficial effects of exercise			X				
Detrimental exercises	X						
General space			X				
Personal space			X				
BODY CONTROL							
Standing Posture	X						
Even beat	X						
Uneven beat		X					
Forward shoulder roll		X	X				
Backward shoulder roll							
LEISURE ACTIVITIES							
PERSONAL/SOCIAL							
Effort	X						
Self discipline		X					
Following directions			X				

* X=Entry Status, O=Exit Status

Figure 9.5. Example student performance score sheet

With an objective-related instructional program in place, the need for student evaluation (with respect to test content) is clear. The performance standards specified or implied in the objectives of the program become the standards of performance to be used in the assessment.

Formats for Reporting Students' Achievements

There are many ways in which evaluation reports may be formulated. Some are lengthy narrative reports, while others are reduced to a single letter or number representing all learning for a given marking period. Each type has strengths and weaknesses which should be considered prior to choosing the most appropriate approach. Among the more popular formats are profiles, letter grades, and narrative reports.

Profile: For objective-related instructional programs, the students' evaluation profile is a direct indication of a student's performance on the objectives of the marking period and/or the program. The profile provides a pictorial representation of the content taught, entry and exit status, and the amount of change for the current instructional period. It may also include information relating to the student's performance to some norm. If the profile was so designed, it would include all of the information necessary to constitute a comprehensive reporting system. See Figure 9-5 for an example of how a profile can be constructed.

All of the data necessary to initiate such a profile can be computerized. The only information that would be needed to print the profile would be the name and entry and/or exit performance level on each objective taught during the reporting period. The remainder of the information, including the student's relative status within the class or other group of reference, would be calculated automatically and printed in response to the student's identification number.

There are many variations of this type of reporting format that could be used for particular situations. The profile, although particularly conducive to computer technology, can also be designed to be completed manually. In instances of manual recording, comparison with peer groups would be left on charts for reference as needed.

Letter grades: Letter grades (i.e., A, B, C, D, F; S, U) have been used for years with a great array of meanings both within and across teachers and districts. Although grades communicate a general level of ability to most individuals, they fail to communicate specific information necessary to effectively report students' progress. No information is provided regarding what content was taught, what the entry or exit performance was on specific objectives, and whether or not the grade represents current status or the changes that were made as the result of instruction.

Because the letter grade is a general indicator, it should be accompanied by explanations of how it was derived and what it represents. If the explanation of the grade is complete, it must make reference to all of the information included in the profile.

Narrative reports: Narrative reports are also completed in many different ways. They range from open-ended general descriptions of how well individual students are doing to highly structured computerized reports that provide selections of many specific statements that can be used to characterize the status of students.

Like letter grades, the statements have general meaning but are often impossible to interpret. Open-ended general descriptors often communicate less than a single letter grade. Somehow, they seem more personal and have consequently found widespread use, particularly in elementary schools. A good narrative report simply converts the information on a good profile into narrative form.

SUMMARY

Student evaluation should be directly related to the objectives of the curriculum. It must incorporate (or have a sound rationale for not incorporating) each of the following elements: the content covered, the student's entry performance level, and indication of the student's exit status and the amounts of change on the objectives included in the reporting period. The student's status relative to peers is also needed. Although many formats for reporting student progress are available, the student profile, as illustrated in this chapter, provides the information necessary for whatever selection is made.

Chapter 10

Program Evaluation

Two of the most important characteristics of an effective objective-related instructional program is that it enables those who initiate it to make systematic changes and it has the structure and procedures that are necessary to demonstrate evidence of its effectiveness. There are three important implications of the above statement:

1. Before a program can be dynamic, it must be definable.
2. In order to remediate weaknesses, some sort of evaluative procedure(s) must be implemented to identify them.
3. Evidence must be obtained to document claims of effectiveness.

The first implication listed above is achieved when an objective-related instructional system is in place. The content that is taught, why it is included in the program, and how it is organized results from completing the steps outlined in Chapters 4, 5, and 6. Chapters 7 and 8 indicate "how" the programs can be implemented in a way that is repeatable while retaining great flexibility. This chapter addresses the second and third implications, that is, in order to improve the program, its strengths and weaknesses must be identified and appropriate revisions made. It also addresses the need to systematically improve the instructional program to generate evidence to back up claims of effectiveness.

PROGRAM EVALUATION DEFINED

Evaluation is a process by which the merit of the program can be determined. The process of evaluation seeks to determine strengths and weaknesses by comparing the program's intents with actual occurrences. Data related to the observed weaknesses will often provide information as to "why" the deficiencies exist and therefore provide valuable insights necessary for needed change.

The need for evaluation is based upon the recognition that programs are never perfect or even acceptable on all counts. Because programs always can be improved, the question becomes one of, "How can appropriate changes be tailored to fit the actual weaknesses of the program without negatively affecting program strengths?"

Program, as the term is used in this chapter, refers to the K-12 physical education program. The procedures can, however, also be applied to instruction related to one program objective, a unit, a year, a program level, or a collection of program levels. Wherever the term "program" is used, it is also appropriate, therefore, to simply substitute the term unit, program objective, year, etc.

PURPOSE OF PROGRAM EVALUATION

As indicated above, the goal of evaluation is to determine merit. The role of evaluation is multifaceted. Teachers can evaluate a total program, a program component, an individual's program, or the program of a particular population group. Similarly, teachers can evaluate the ends of a program, the means to the ends, or the degree to which the program meets some external standards. The more common purposes of evaluation are listed below.

1. To document the validity and/or importance of the expectations (goals, objectives) of the program
2. To document the way in which the program is being implemented
3. To determine the effect of the program on its participants
4. To provide information-based recommendations for revisions necessary to reduce identified weaknesses

The application of evaluation procedures can provide results that are as numerous and varied as the roles that evaluation can serve. This chapter advocates concentrating evaluation methods to provide evidence for: 1) program improvement and 2) program effectiveness.

EVALUATION FOR PROGRAM IMPROVEMENT

Evaluation for the improvement of local programs should proceed from an initial self-study of program characteristics and perceived outcomes to a data-based study of characteristics and outcomes. Too frequently, the process of program evaluation begins and ends with the completion of a series of checklists that pertain to teacher-pupil ratios, space for activities, class size, and balance in program objectives. Such a process concludes with the assumption that more could be accomplished if the available resources were not so restricted. What is so blatantly missing in such an evaluation is any attempt to determine whether the instructional program changed the motor, psychological, and physical characteristics of the students. Until such evidence is available, there can be no claim of program effectiveness.

One of the most useful processes inherent in the development of exemplary physical education programs is a self-study that school districts should initiate prior to conducting an evaluation of program effectiveness. The self-study provides an opportunity to subject the program to a series of standard criteria in an effort to improve the program prior to conducting an evaluation of program effectiveness.

Appendix C provides an instrument that may be used by school districts to guide a self-study of the merits and deficiencies in their existing programs. The appendix also contains a sequence of procedures that may be helpful in initiating and conducting the study, and reporting and acting on the information obtained.

A review of the instrument will reveal its structure. Essentially there are 15 categories of information provided for conducting the self-study. Each category has several items which are to be rated by members of the self-study team. These items should be considered indicators of program merit in the category. As suggested in the implementation procedures, the self-study team members representing physical education staff, building and central administration, parents and, where appropriate, students, should independently complete the checklist. Consensus should then be obtained with a re-rating of items after a discussion of individual ratings and their rationale. Aggregation of the items by category then provides the information necessary to generate a report and recommendations for future action. Often a self-study will reveal the need for significant work directed at program improvement which should be completed prior to initiating the more costly, difficult task of conducting an evaluation of program effectiveness.

EVALUATION FOR PROGRAM EFFECTIVENESS

There are currently many models available to guide educational evaluations. Most are well described in the evaluation literature and, more recently, examples of their use have been published as an aid to the design of similar evaluation studies. Most of the available models cannot be readily used by teachers because they are too complex and are usually written generically to be used in a wide variety of educational settings. Consequently it is often difficult to make application to a specific, local programmatic need. More important, their complexity is overwhelming not only from the standpoint of evaluation design but also from the standpoint of the time required for their implementation. Teachers simply do not have the time necessary to conduct a formal evaluation as described in most models. Accordingly, the help of an evaluation specialist is necessary to design and conduct an evaluation of program effectiveness.

Program evaluation appropriate to an objective-related instructional system as described here should be designed to answer two basic questions.

1. Is the program producing the intended outcomes?
2. How can the program be improved to be more effective or efficient?

The steps which follow describe an overview of the procedures that can be used to answer these questions.

Assuming that the program is well-defined; has been judged appropriate in terms of its characteristics related to content, structure, and implementation; and is repeatable (prerequisite characteristics identified in the self-study) the next question becomes:

Was the program implemented as intended?

Program Implementation

Before any attempt is made to assess the degree to which students made important gains, it is necessary to define how the program was implemented. Several considerations are of particular interest.

1. Are the students enrolled in the program representative of the type (age, gender, background) of students for whom the program was planned?
2. Is the program being implemented by the type of teachers (classroom, physical education specialists, consultants, volunteers, aides, others) in the teacher-student ratios for which the program was designed?
3. Has the content (program objectives) planned for inclusion in the program been taught?
4. Has the amount of instructional time planned for each program objective been allotted to its instruction?
5. Was the planned sequence (within and across objectives) implemented?
6. Have the procedures for implementation been conducted as defined in the program's implementation plan?

Unless there is evidence that aspects such as those listed above have been instituted, it must be acknowledged that some undefined version of the program rather than the defined program is being evaluated. If the program has been modified from the original pre-implementation plans, it is not critical. The critical point is that whatever was implemented is known and described well enough to be repeated.

Obtaining evidence of how the program was implemented can be accomplished by special monitoring. Describing the specifics of this process is beyond the scope of this book. The procedure is, however, described in the evaluation literature.

Where there are discrepancies between the program's actual implementation and desired implementation, it may be necessary to institute the appropriate corrective actions. Although the primary objective of the evaluation is to determine if the program is effective, information about the program's implementation must be available for two important reasons:

1. When it is learned that the program has resulted in important student gains, a good description of the implementation process increases the possibility that the instructional activities could be replicated for the benefit of other groups of students.

2. Where the results of implementation of the unit did not meet the expectation levels (in terms of student gains), one could look for characteristics of the program's implementation that were deficient in an attempt to identify appropriate program modifications.

If, during the course of the program's implementation, it becomes apparent that changes must be made to facilitate or even allow planned implementation to occur, they can and should be made. Accumulations of such refinements cause the program to grow in its effectiveness. They are the desirable products of evaluation activity.

Where there is no adequate description of the program, constant refinement and growth is not possible. Years of refinement associated with an excellent instructor who leaves the system are lost because they were never incorporated into the description of the program. A successor must start all over to build the program without the benefit of information learned and previously included in the program. Such an occurrence is a tremendous waste of public resources and a serious disservice to the students of the district.

Program Effectiveness

Evaluation of the program is merely an extension of the evaluation of individual students. Evaluation of individual students within an objective-related instructional system is straightforward in that the program's organization, implementation, and evaluation are based upon program objectives. Program evaluation seeks to describe the number of students enrolled in the program who are making important gains on the objectives taught. If the proportion of gains is large enough, then we say the program is effective; if insufficient gains occur, then we conclude the program needs revision.

Criteria for Establishing Evidence of Effectiveness

Several criteria must be met before it can be claimed that a program is effective. Briefly, these include:[1]

1. Did a change occur?

   - Was the change central to the claim of effectiveness?
   - Was the measurement valid and reliable?

2. Was the change statistically significant?

---

1 *Modified from Tallmadge (1977).*

3. Was the effect educationally significant?
   - Was the size of the effect(s) large enough?
   - Is the effect(s) important?
   - Was the cost/benefit ratio of the effect(s) desirable?
4. Can the effect(s) be replicated in another setting?
   - Can replication occur in the same or similar situations?
   - Can replication occur at another point in time?
   - Can replication occur with different staffing?
5. Did the observed effect(s) result from the program?
   - Was the validity of the design (internal and external) sufficient?
6. Is the evidence believable?
   - Were the data complete, carefully collected and coded?
   - Are appropriate descriptive statistics reported?
   - Are the procedures for data collection and analysis sufficiently described?
   - Are the limitations of the study presented?

Earlier we implied that information collected to test for evidence of effectiveness should be completed on relatively small samples of students that are representative of the rest of the enrolled students. Implementation of this recommendation provides the means to obtain the measurement rigor (reliability and validity) required to obtain believable data. It is also appropriate to sample program objectives from those included in the program. The type of reduction in student numbers and the amount of content included in the design of the evaluation provides for obtaining high quality data and believable results while maintaining a reasonable work load for those involved in the evaluation activity.

A full description of the procedures necessary to conduct an evaluation of program effectiveness goes far beyond that which can be included in this book. There is, however, a great deal of literature available to those interested in program evaluation that provides the specifications necessary to conduct quality program evaluations. The following paragraphs provide an overview of the evaluation steps and procedures necessary to generate evidence of program effectiveness that will meet the aforementioned criteria.

These include:

1. Clearly identify the purpose of the program.
   a. Goals and objectives.
   b. Implementation procedures.
2. Develop the evaluation questions that will guide the evaluation process.
3. Develop a design and sampling plan that provides appropriate control for sources of internal and external invalidity for each evaluation question.
4. Select, adapt, and/or develop reliable and valid instruments to measure the outcomes of the program.
5. Establish data collection procedures that specify who will collect the data, how it will be collected, from whom it will be procured, and at what time.
6. Develop a management system for handling, coding, and storing data that will maximize its integrity and minimize manipulation costs.
7. Develop a data analysis plan that will provide the appropriate descriptive and inferential statistics necessary to answer each evaluation question.
8. Develop an evaluation report format for presenting the evaluation methodology, the data, and interpretations.
9. Implement the evaluation plans.
10. Report the obtained results, by evaluation question, to the appropriate audience.

When the above steps have been implemented and the criteria for evidence of effectiveness met, it is appropriate to claim exemplary status for a program. Until such criteria are met, advocates for a program must admit that although the program meets appropriate professional standards (*i.e.*, criteria from a typical checklist), evidence of its effectiveness is not available. The right to claim effectiveness, and back up the claim with data, puts the program staff in a position to actively communicate the benefits of the program to its sponsors. It also places the staff in a strong position to request the resources necessary to obtain other important, but lower priority program objectives. Without such data, the program will remain vulnerable to erosion during periods of financial difficulty or when administrative leadership is changed.

Although having evidence of effectiveness is highly desirable, it is not the only benefit of program evaluation. Generation of evidence of effectiveness will always point out strengths and weaknesses of a program.

Description of the Program in Terms of Strengths and Weaknesses

Determining what aspects of the program have not been effective in producing meaningful student gains provide important information for program improvement. Wherever expectations have not been met, the staff and evaluation team need to determine why and initiate appropriate changes.

Determining needed changes: Having the results of the program described in terms of strengths and weaknesses is necessary to initiate program improvements, but it is not sufficient to make appropriate changes. Knowledge of what to improve must be supplemented with information suggesting "why" the weakness exists. Only by identifying why an identified weakness has occurred can we formulate recommendations for revision that are likely to change that weakness into a strength.

A weakness observed in program implementation usually results from a lack of knowledge about the process that is necessary for planning, implementing, and/or evaluating. This interpretation suggests the need for specific inservice education designed to remedy the observed deficiency in implementation.

The determination of why a sufficient number of students have not made meaningful gains on one or more of the program's objectives is a much more difficult task. There is, however, an approach that can be used to obtain answers to this question. It involves investigating the relationships between student outcomes and other variables.

Several categories of variables are used.

1. Characteristics of the students
2. Characteristics of the teachers
3. Characteristics of the instructional setting or context
4. Characteristics of the program's implementation

By studying the strength of the relationship between these "inputs" and the programs "outcomes," insight is often gained regarding potential revisions. The stronger the relationship between student outcomes and variables or group of variables, the more likely that the reason(s) for achievement may be attributed to the identified variable.

This type of analysis can be productive in identifying potential causes for why a weakness in achievement was identified. From these analyses potential changes emerge which must be developed, implemented, and re-evaluated. As changes are identified and remediated, program effectiveness and efficiency are improved. Refinement refers to either improving effectiveness or maintaining effectiveness while reducing the amount of resources (*i.e.*, time) consumed. If resources can be reduced, then additional program objectives can be added to the program.

It is critical that recommended changes be included in an updated description of the program. Only when the program is sufficiently described can it be systematically changed and/or replicated in other settings.

SUMMARY

Program evaluation is necessary to obtain evidence of effectiveness and to systematically improve the curriculum and instruction. Both self-study and evaluation of program effectiveness contribute to those outcomes. It must be remembered that programs must be sufficiently described so that their key components can be replicated when found effective, or systematically changed when found ineffective or inefficient. Evaluation in a self-study format can be conducted without professional assistance, whereas evaluation of program effectiveness will typically require the assistance of an evaluator. Both evaluation procedures contribute to program improvement. Claims for program effectiveness, however, can only be made in the presence of data which verify student outcomes in accordance with stringent evaluative criteria.

References

Brophy, J.E. and Evertson, C. (1976). *Learning from teaching: A developmental perspective.* Boston, MA: Allyn and Bacon.

Bruner, J. (1981, August). On instructability. Paper presented at the meeting of the American Psychological Association, Los Angeles, CA.

Carmichael, D.L. & Vogel, P.G. (1978). Research into practice. *Journal of Physical Education and Recreation, 49*(3), 29-30.

Crandall, D.P., & Loucks, S.F. (1983). *A roadmap for school improvement: Executive summary of the study of dissemination efforts supporting school improvement.* Andover, MA: The Network.

Davis, R.H. (1977). Learning by design. *New Directions for Higher Education, 17,* 17-31.

Fisher, C.W., Berliner, D.C., Filby, N.N., Marliave, R.S., Cahen, L.S., and Dishaw, M.M. (1980). Teaching behaviors, Academic Learning time and student achievement: An overview. In C. Denham and A. Lieberman (Eds.) *Time to learn.* Washington, D.C.: US Department of Education, National Institute of Education.

Fisher, C.W., Filby, N.N., Marliave, R.S., Cahen, L.S., Dishaw, M.M., Moore, J.E., and Berliner, D.C. (1978). Teaching behaviors, academic learning time, and student achievement. Final report of Phase III-B, Beginning teacher evaluation study, Technical report. San Francisco, CA: Far West Laboratory for Educational Research and Development.

Huberman, M.A. & Crandall, D.P. (1982). *People, policies, and practices: Examining the chain of school improvement - Implications for action.* Andover, MA: The Network.

Loucks, S.F., Cox, P.L., Miles, M.B., Huberman, M.A., & Eiseman, J.W. (1982). *People, policies, and practices: Examining the chain of school improvement - Portraits of the changes, the players, and the contexts.* Andover, MA: The Network.

National Association of Elementary School Principals (1984). *Standards for quality elementary schools: Kindergarten through eighth grade.* Reston, VA: Author.

Rosenshine, B.V. (1983). Teaching functions in instructional programs. *The Elementary School Journal, 83,* 335-352.

Rowe, M.B. (1974). Wait time and rewards as instructional variables: Their influence on language, logic, and fate control. Part one, Wait time. *Journal of Research in Science Teaching, 11*, 81-94.

Rutter, M., Maugham, B., Mortmore, P., and Ousten, J. (1979). *Fifteen thousand hours*. Cambridge, MA: Harvard University Press.

Seefeldt, V. D. (Ed.), (1986). *Physical activity and well- being*, Reston, VA: American Alliance for Health, Physical Education, Recreation and Dance.

Seefeldt, V. D. and Vogel, P. G. (1986). *The value of physical activity*, Reston, VA: American Alliance for Health, Physical Education, Recreation and Dance.

Tallmadge, G. K. (1977). *Ideabook: Joint dissemination review panel*. Washington, DC: Superintendent of Documents, U. S. Government Printing Office.

Vogel, P. G. (1979, Fall). Systematic program design: Evaluation. *Wyoming Journal of Health, Physical Education and Recreation*.

Webb, N.M. (1980). A process-outcome analysis of learning in group and individual settings. *Educational Psychologist, 15*, 69-83.

Appendix A

Criteria For Program Evaluation

1. **Program Purpose:** The intended outcomes of the physical education program are stated as goals that represent documented evidence of the relationship between physical activity, health and performance.

   Interpretation: Program goals must represent more than a broad, general statement of instructional intent. They must express a belief about what can and should be the purpose of a physical education program, and clearly be related to the evidence that enumerates the contributions of activity to human well-being. Goal statements are written as outcomes (*i.e.*, they represent the results of instruction, rather than the process of instruction).

2. **Relevant Goals:** Goals are proposed by professional educators, through consultation with community representatives, to ensure relevance of content to local situations.

   Interpretation: This criterion measures the degree to which the content of the program, as stated in the goals, represents outcomes that are viewed as important and relevant by representatives of the local community. Such information should be obtained from administrators, teachers, parents, students, school board members, and others. It should then be used to finalize the goals and/or the relative emphasis the goals are to receive while implementing the physical education program.

3. **Program Objectives:** Each goal is accompanied by program objectives which define the content by which the goal is achieved.

   Interpretation: This criterion seeks to measure the useability of goals. Every goal statement should be divided into a number of program objectives. Program objectives identify specific outcomes that students seek to achieve, and therefore, serve as elements of program content that can be sequenced within and across each level of a K-12 program. Achievement of the program objectives (which operationally define the meaning of the goal) indicates that the goal was achieved.

4. **Curriculum Structure:** The sequential organization of program objectives into a K-12 curriculum structure involves the participation of teachers and administrators representing each level of the program.

   Interpretation: Sequentially arranging program objectives according to student needs and their level of complexity is an essential step in organizing the curriculum. The scope and sequence which result ensure that students receive instruction on important content without unnecessary repetition or inappropriate expectations. The K-12 curriculum organization should represent decisions made by teachers and administrators who are familiar with the learners' needs and characteristics at each specific grade level. Personnel at the various grade levels are also knowledgeable concerning time allotments for physical education, facility and space conditions, and other unique environmental factors that affect curricular decisions.

5. **Instructional Objectives:** Program objectives are translated into a logical sequence of instructional objectives.

   Interpretation: Instructional objectives define specific levels of achievement within each program objective and are stated in terms which promote reliable assessment. They serve as sequential targets for instruction, as well as indicators of student achievement. The first instructional objective in a sequence is an appropriate objective for students with little ability, while the last instructional objective in the sequence defines mastery of the content named in the program objective.

6. **Instructional Time:** Program objectives included at each grade level are finalized by eliminating the discrepancies between the instructional time needed to achieve expected student outcomes and the time available for instruction.

   Interpretation: Physical educators have made claims about accomplishing a wide variety of goals and objectives in the schools. Recently, schools have been asked to improve or maintain effectiveness while program resources (time, money, staff, equipment, and others) have been reduced. Critics have also become more vocal in expressing the ineffectiveness of school programs in meeting purposeful goals and objectives. Because effectiveness is judged in terms of student outcomes, the amount of time assigned to each instructional objective must be sufficient to result in students' achievement of the stated objectives. Where resources are insufficient to effectively teach all desirable program objectives, the number of program objectives included must be reduced in accordance with their relative priorities.

7. **Program Implementation:** Instructors implement the K-12 program in accordance with the curricular plan.

   Interpretation: The curriculum defines the "what," "when," and "why" of physical education. Instruction provides an answer to "how" the objectives are to be attained. Curriculum structure specifies the content, scope, and sequence of objectives. Program objectives are sequenced in both horizontal (throughout the year) and vertical (throughout the grades) dimensions. Instructional objectives are sequenced to specify levels of student achievement and thus transcend horizontal and vertical sequencing in accordance with student growth toward mastery. Instructors at each level of the K-12 program must teach in accordance with the stated curricular plan.

8. **Instructional Guidelines:** Student learning is facilitated by adherence to guidelines drawn from research on teaching effectiveness.

   Interpretation: Designing an environment for effective learning is critical to successful instruction. Recent research on teaching has confirmed many of the traditional techniques of teaching and provided new guidelines on how to improve instruction. Effective teaching should be consistent with such procedures as setting realistic expectations, establishing an orderly and positive environment, grouping according to ability, maximizing feedback and on-task time, maximizing the success rate, monitoring progress, asking appropriate questions, and promoting a sense of student self-control. Instruction in physical education must reflect these guidelines to be effective and efficient.

9. **Student Evaluation:** Students' achievement of instructional objectives is available, in written form, for interpretation to students, parents, staff, administrators, and/or others.

   Interpretation: A written assessment of students' achievement provides the necessary, tangible evidence relating students' progress to specific objectives. The rate of students' progress toward achieving program objectives, in comparison with self and peers, is essential information for program interpretation, subsequent planning, student motivation, and program revision.

10. **Program Evaluation:** Insufficient student attainment of instructional objectives results in subsequent program revision.

Interpretation: Evidence that objectives were not achieved indicates that adjustments must be made prior to subsequent attempts to achieve the same objectives. Lack of achievement can be attributed to various reasons including unreasonable expectations, insufficient entry competencies, inappropriate instructional strategies, and/or insufficient time. Each of these conditions requires program revisions, accompanied by systematic re-evaluation of the changes and their related outcomes.

Appendix B

Guidelines for Effective Educational Change

Effective program redesign and inservice education are most likely to occur when they are implemented in accordance with guidelines drawn from research information that describes effective educational change. The following statements highlight the critical aspects of that research:

- Change should be initiated at the point of need
- Lasting change requires the involvement of representatives of the teaching staff, administration, and community
- Change requires administrative support
- Educational change requires a long-term commitment
- Change best occurs by using a systematic process
- Change requires effective leadership
- Meaningful changes provide evidence of educational effectiveness

Initiated at the point of need: Attempts to redesign the K-12 physical education program are most likely to succeed when they are initiated at a time when there is a clear need (Crandall & Loucks, 1983). Unfortunately, the need is often not recognized until there is significant erosion of the program and/or staff. Astute school administrators and school boards will recognize the need for change in program content or staff competencies before erosion has occurred and will then initiate actions to correct the deficiencies.

Involvement of staff administration and community: Programmatic inservice education attempts that fail to involve representatives of the staff, administration (both building and central), and members of the community are doomed. Involvement is most effective when members from the preceding groups are engaged in face-to-face contact during the planning, implementation, and evaluation of the program and the inservice. This sharing of information, criteria, and processes promotes ownership of, and committment to, the product (Crandall & Loucks,1983). Without this commitment there is little chance that a curriculum product or instructional process will endure.

Administrative support: Administrative support is a prerequisite to effective inservice education (Loucks, Cox, Miles, Huberman & Eiseman, 1982). Such support must be visible in at least two ways. First, the project must be funded. Without a financial commitment there is little reason to believe that the project has captured the interest of the administrators in charge. This does not mean that every project must be staffed and budgeted as a full-time operation. It does mean, however, that monies should be made available to teachers for released time, purchase of appropriate reference materials, and/or consultant assistance as needed. Second, and equally as important as funding, is support in the form of administrative participation in the decision-making activities of the project. Without such participation, the ownership needed to obtain the resources necessary to implement the program may be unavailable.

Long-term commitment: Programmatic inservice that focuses on altering a significant number of needs in content identification, organization, implementation, or evaluation requires a long-term commitment in order to be effective (Crandall & Loucks, 1983). A systematic approach to planning that will gain the confidence of program supporters and/or skeptics cannot be completed in a short time period (*i.e.*, one summer or one year). Rather, a long-term project that provides for systematic design, followed by implementation, evaluation, refinement, re-implementation, and re-evaluation is necessary. It is this long-term cooperative commitment to problem identification and resolution that holds so much potential for the improvement of both public school programs and university preservice and inservice programming.

Systematic process: The use of systematic instructional design procedures is an important adjunct to programmatic inservice efforts (Carmichael & Vogel, 1978; Davis, 1977). Foremost in the application of such procedures is the retrieval and application of scientific information. The scientific information can be used by systematically identifying its implications, applying them to the design of instructional processes or products, implementing and evaluating their effectiveness, refining weaknesses, and recycling through the above steps as necessary to obtain an effective product.

Effective leadership: Effective programmatic inservice education cannot occur without effective leadership. This leadership must be personal, credible, and sensitive, while at the same time being forceful, if necessary, to maintain order and progress (Huberman & Crandell, 1982; Sergiovanni, 1984).

Evidence of effectiveness: Participation in a long-term cooperative programmatic project must result in evidence of effectiveness. There must be a convincing argument that can be offered in support of what is included as content in the program, why it is organized in a certain way, and why the principles or guidelines used to implement instruction are important. Of most importance is the ability to provide evidence that a significant number of students achieved meaningful changes in performance on a significant number of the programs objectives. Of similar importance is the capability of replicating the program with other students and in other years. Without the ability to replicate there is no evidence of the existence of a "program." Rather, one must concede that the "program" (with or without evidence of effectiveness) can at best be identified as a one- time educational event.

References

Carmichael, D.L. & Vogel, P.G. (1978). Research into practice. *Journal of Physical Education and Recreation, 49*(3), 29-30.

Crandall, D.P., & Loucks, S.F. (1983). *A roadmap for school improvement: Executive summary of the study of dissemination efforts supporting school improvement.* Andover, MA: The Network.

Davis, R.H. (1977). Learning by design. *New Directions for Higher Education, 17,*17-31.

Huberman, M.A. & Crandall, D.P. (1982). *People, policies, and practices: Examining the chain of school improvement - Implications for action.* Andover, MA: The Network.

Loucks, S.F., Cox, P.L., Miles, M.B., Huberman, M.A., & Eiseman, J.W. (1982). *People, policies, and practices: Examining the chain of school improvement - Portraits of the changes, the players, and the contexts.* Andover, MA: The Network.

Appendix C

Materials for Conducting a Self-study

> **The materials in this appendix include:**
> 1. Recommended steps for conducting a self-study
> 2. A self-study instrument
> 3. Suggested prerequisites for initiating an evaluation to determine program effectiveness
> 4. A sample reporting format

Recommended Steps for Conducting a Self-study

1. Review the self-study materials and procedures and decide whether or not to initiate the study.
2. Obtain necessary approvals from the district administration.
3. Carefully outline the procedures to be followed.
4. Establish the self-study team.
    A. Local representatives
        Administration
        Classroom teachers
        Physical education staff
        Parents
        Selected others
    B. Consultant representation from outside the district
5. Prepare the self-study team to conduct the study.
    A. Overview the purpose and the procedures
    B. Review the instrument
6. Complete the self-study in accordance with the established procedures.
7. Develop a consensus report of program status for each category of the self-study checklist.
8. Self-study team and the consultant develop recommendations for action.
    A. Program improvement
    B. Evaluation of effectiveness
9. Report self-study findings to the full physical education staff and to the district administration.

Appendix C   C - 3

                    Name: _____

                    Representing:_____

                    Building(s) _____

                    Grade Level(s): K 1 2 3 4 5 6 7 8 9 10 11 12

                                     (circle)

A CHECKLIST TO AID IN THE SELF-STUDY
OF PROGRAMS OF PHYSICAL EDUCATION*

* *Prepared for use in the Michigan Exemplary Physical Education Program Project, Michigan Association for Health, Physical Education, Recreation and Dance, Paul Vogel and Vern Seefeldt, Co Directors*

This checklist covers 15 categories of information that can be used to describe characteristics of a program, its staff and clients, and the context within which it operates. Each category contains several indicators of quality that have been linked to effective schooling. Although the checklist has been developed to describe characteristics associated with the delivery of physical education services, it includes categories (and indicators) that describe not only physical education but the context within which the physical education program exists. The checklist was purposely developed to be compatible in content, form, and outcomes with the National Association of Elementary School Principals "Standards for Quality Elementary Schools: Kindergarten through Eighth Grade" to facilitate joint school and program improvement efforts.[1] The 15 categories of information are:

Program goals and objectives
Curriculum organization
Implementation of instruction
Student evaluation
Program evaluation
Qualified personnel
K-12 leadership
Building leadership

Teacher evaluation
Professional development
School climate
Student characteristics
Teacher characteristics
Public relations
Safety and medical requirements

In each of the above categories several indicators of quality schools are listed. These indicators are formatted in a way that allows them to be rated in terms of the degree to which you agree or disagree with each statement.

Completed reactions to the quality indicators can be used in two ways. First, low ratings can signal the need to initiate program improvements necessary to convert perceived weaknesses into strengths. Second, evidence of insufficient student achievement of a program's objectives compared with ratings on the indicators can reveal program characteristics that may account for low student achievement. In both situations program characteristics can be improved, thereby increasing the possibility of improving student achievement.

---

[1] *Modified from NAESP (1984), Standards for elementary schools, and Vogel (1979), Systematic program design: Eva*

Appendix C C - 5

SELF-STUDY CHECKLIST

Rate the degree to which your program is characterized by the items in each of the following categories. Circle one of the following responses:

SD = strongly disagree
D = disagree
N = neutral
A = agree
SA = strongly agree

Program Goals and Objectives

1. Written program goals are available for review.   SD   D   N   A   SA
2. Program goals represent the potential contributions of activity to well-being.   SD   D   N   A   SA
3. Program goals represent both professional and community values to assure their local relevance.   SD   D   N   A   SA
4. Program goals are known by staff and administrators.   SD   D   N   A   SA
5. Program goals are stated in student outcome terminology rather than instructional input terminology.   SD   D   N   A   SA
6. The physical education program goals are consistent with district educational goals.   SD   D   N   A   SA
7. Written and measurable objectives are specified for each program goal.   SD   D   N   A   SA
8. Objectives are divided into a range of instructional levels that represent low to high degrees of student mastery.   SD   D   N   A   SA

Curriculum Organization

1. Objectives that define each goal are organized into a logical progression K-12.   SD   D   N   A   SA
2. The K-12 progression was developed using the expertise of teachers and administrators representing each level of the program.   SD   D   N   A   SA
3. Objectives included at a particular grade level are further organized into a logical teaching order.   SD   D   N   A   SA
4. The number of objectives included at each level of the program represents a match between the time needed for a majority of the students to make an important gain and the amount of time available for instruction.   SD   D   N   A   SA
5. The program goals and objectives represent all of the physical education content included in the K-12 program.   SD   D   N   A   SA
6. Curriculum objectives are appropriate for the grade levels in which they appear.   SD   D   N   A   SA
7. There are objectives in the curriculum within each of the following broad categories of content:
   fitness   SD   D   N   A   SA
   skill   SD   D   N   A   SA
   knowledge   SD   D   N   A   SA
   personal/social content categories   SD   D   N   A   SA

Implementation of Instruction

1. Instructors at each level of the program are teaching objectives in accordance with the K-12 plan.   SD   D   N   A   SA
2. Instructional materials and activities are directly related to the objectives of the curriculum.   SD   D   N   A   SA
3. Class time is used for appropriate learning tasks.   SD   D   N   A   SA
4. Interruptions to other scheduled classes are minimal.   SD   D   N   A   SA
5. Lessons are implemented in accordance with daily lesson plans.   SD   D   N   A   SA
6. Students are assembled for instruction according to need, ranging from individual to whole class groupings.   SD   D   N   A   SA
7. Teachers demonstrate thorough understanding of effective instructional procedures.   SD   D   N   A   SA
8. Teachers use informal evaluation techniques to guide appropriate feedback to students.   SD   D   N   A   SA
9. Teachers provide sufficient opportunities for students to practice and acquire stated objectives.   SD   D   N   A   SA
10. Specific, immediate and constructive feedback is regularly given during instruction.   SD   D   N   A   SA
11. Students with special needs are identified and the proper support is provided.   SD   D   N   A   SA
12. Class management results in an orderly but comfortable environment.   SD   D   N   A   SA
13. Students are expected to give their "best efforts."   SD   D   N   A   SA
14. Minimal instructional time is lost to taking attendance, changing locations, forming and changing groups, changing from one activity to another, altering facilities, and dispensing equipment.   SD   D   N   A   SA
15. Homework related to the achievement of curriculum objectives is assigned and monitored where appropriate.   SD   D   N   A   SA
16. Instruction is guided (assessment and prescription) by student status on clearly stated instructional objectives.   SD   D   N   A   SA
17. Standard class routines are explicitly taught to the students in the first few days of class.   SD   D   N   A   SA
18. Student-teacher ratios are consistent with those recommended for other curriculum content areas.   SD   D   N   A   SA

Student Evaluation

1. Student achievement of the instructional objectives is observed and recorded.   SD   D   N   A   SA
2. Student achievement levels are known and used by the K-12 staff for program planning.   SD   D   N   A   SA
3. Results of student achievement are incorporated into instructional plans for subsequent lessons.   SD   D   N   A   SA
4. Reports to students and parents clearly portray the objectives, status and progress of the students.   SD   D   N   A   SA

Appendix C   C - 7

5. Students' status relative to their peers is available   SD   D   N   A   SA
   upon request.

6. Student status relative to important criterion per-   SD   D   N   A   SA
   formance levels is reported to students and parents.

Program Evaluation

1. A written plan for regularly evaluating the K-12   SD   D   N   A   SA
   program exists.
2. The degree to which the objectives of the program   SD   D   N   A   SA
   are attained by students is annually reported
   and available for review.
3. The degree to which the objectives of the program   SD   D   N   A   SA
   are attained by students is used for program revision.
4. Data collection procedures result in obtaining   SD   D   N   A   SA
   valid and reliable data.
5. Program evaluation includes both self-study and   SD   D   N   A   SA
   external review.
6. Appropriate comparison groups are used to   SD   D   N   A   SA
   accurately interpret results of program evaluation.
7. Evaluation results are available to interested mem-   SD   D   N   A   SA
   bers of the community.
8. There is a strong written rationale supporting   SD   D   N   A   SA
   the test instruments used in the evaluation.
9. There is convincing evidence that the instructional   SD   D   N   A   SA
   program is described well enough that
   it can be replicated by other teachers
   in other schools in other years.
10. There is convincing evidence that a sufficient
    number of the students are making significant
    gains on a majority of the programs objectives
    in the following goal areas:
        fitness   SD   D   N   A   SA
        skill   SD   D   N   A   SA
        knowledge   SD   D   N   A   SA
        personal/social   SD   D   N   A   SA
11. Teachers use formal assessment of students' pro-   SD   D   N   A   SA
    gress to evaluate program effectiveness.
12. Where evidence of program ineffectiveness is   SD   D   N   A   SA
    obtained, the reasons for these deficiencies are
    systematically sought.
13. Changes in the program of instruction are   SD   D   N   A   SA
    regularly made on the basis of this evidence (cited
    in number 12).
14. Changes in the methods of instruction are   SD   D   N   A   SA
    regularly made on the basis of this evidence (cited
    in number 12).

Qualified Personnel

1. Staff members are qualified (education and   SD   D   N   A   SA
   background) for their teaching assignments.

2. Appropriate support staff (*i.e.*, secretaries, custodians, aides) are available to the physical education staff.   SD D N A SA
3. Volunteers regularly participate in the physical education instructional program.   SD D N A SA
4. Other professional staff are available to physical education students based on individual needs (*i. e.* school psychologists, counselors, nurses, special educators, social workers).   SD D N A SA
5. The physical education faculty have a current and comprehensive understanding of:
   a. the contributions of physical activity to well-being   SD D N A SA
   b. the relationship between the potential contributions of activity and program goals and objectives   SD D N A SA
   c. the substance and rationale for the programs K-12 organization   SD D N A SA
   d. guidelines for effective instruction   SD D N A SA
   e. the relationship between program goals and objectives and student evaluation procedures   SD D N A SA
   f. how to evaluate and improve the program   SD D N A SA

K-12 Leadership

1. The K-12 curriculum and instructional procedures are monitored to assure their use in the physical education program.   SD D N A SA
2. The instructional materials are sufficient to meet curricular needs.   SD D N A SA
3. The equipment is sufficient to meet curricular needs.   SD D N A SA
4. The facilities are sufficient to meet curricular needs.   SD D N A SA
5. The administrator charged with annually reporting on the quality of the physical education program, K-12, is known to all.   SD D N A SA

Building(s) Leadership

1. The principal exemplifies the Code of Ethics endorsed by the National Association of School Principals.   SD D N A SA
2. The principal can articulate the value of exemplary physical education programs.   SD D N A SA
3. The principal conveys high expectations both for staff and students.   SD D N A SA
4. The principal is characterized by:
   a. self-confidence   SD D N A SA
   b. respect and appreciation of others   SD D N A SA
   c. recognizing the accomplishments of others   SD D N A SA
   d. openness to logical change   SD D N A SA

Appendix C   C - 9

      e. initiative   SD   D   N   A   SA
      f. enthusiasm   SD   D   N   A   SA

5. The principal facilitates the implementation   SD   D   N   A   SA
    of the K-12 curriculum.
6. The principal facilitates the use of guidelines for   SD   D   N   A   SA
    effective instruction.
7. The top priority of the principal is teaching   SD   D   N   A   SA
    excellence.
8. A system for evaluating principals which is   SD   D   N   A   SA
    similar in scope to that suggested for evaluating
    teachers is in place.

Teacher Evaluation

1. There is a teacher evaluation plan including   SD   D   N   A   SA
    specific procedures and performance criteria in place.
2. Teacher evaluation is based on student achieve-   SD   D   N   A   SA
    ment, observation of practice, and alteration of
    practices deemed insufficient on prior observations.
3. Evaluation is viewed as a positive, cooperative   SD   D   N   A   SA
    team approach (teacher and evaluator) to
    improving instruction.
4. The evaluation process is effective in distinguishing   SD   D   N   A   SA
    between effective and ineffective instruction
    and perhaps more importantly, results in
    recommendations for improvement.
5. Resources are assigned to teacher improvement.   SD   D   N   A   SA
6. Written procedures exist that meet legal   SD   D   N   A   SA
    requirements for dismissing incompetent teachers.
7. A reward system for teaching excellence and   SD   D   N   A   SA
    improvement is in place.

Professional Development

1. A staff development program for physical   SD   D   N   A   SA
    educators exists and is based on needs identified
    through evaluation of the program and its
    instructional procedures.
2. The staff routinely obtains information repre-   SD   D   N   A   SA
    senting research on effective schooling.
3. The inservice education program is built on   SD   D   N   A   SA
    knowledge of effective adult education practices
    and is relevant to assigned responsibilities.
4. Resources assigned to staff development   SD   D   N   A   SA
    provide for sufficient inservice education both
    within and outside the school day.
5. The staff develoment program is evaluated and   SD   D   N   A   SA
    revised in accordance with identified deficiencies.
6. Staff development provides opportunities for   SD   D   N   A   SA
    teachers to observe and coach others on
    effective schooling practices.
7. Financial resources and time (at least 10 days)   SD   D   N   A   SA

    are available annually for planning, staff development, conferences, or workshops.
 8. The staff is involved in professional organizations at the local, state, and/or national level.   SD   D   N   A   SA

School Climate

 1. School-community interaction is planned.   SD   D   N   A   SA
 2. School-community interaction is evaluated.   SD   D   N   A   SA
 3. Eighty percent of the parents would say they feel welcome and comfortable in the school.   SD   D   N   A   SA
 4. Parents and teachers work cooperatively to plan and to instruct students.   SD   D   N   A   SA
 5. Parent education programs are regularly offered.   SD   D   N   A   SA
 6. Faculty members are committed to the mission of the school.   SD   D   N   A   SA
 7. Administrative staff members are committed to the mission of the school.   SD   D   N   A   SA
 8. There is mutual respect between students and school personnel.   SD   D   N   A   SA
 9. Conflict resolution practices are defined, fair and consistently applied.   SD   D   N   A   SA
 10. Facilities and equipment are well-maintained (*i.e.*, aesthetic, safe, clean).   SD   D   N   A   SA
 11. There is a written code of conduct for students that is consistently implemented.   SD   D   N   A   SA
 12. Students, teachers, parents and administrators share the responsibility for discipline.   SD   D   N   A   SA
 13. Accomplishments of faculty and staff are appropriately recognized.   SD   D   N   A   SA
 14. Accomplishments of students are appropriately recognized.   SD   D   N   A   SA
 15. Students and staff recognize that outstanding performance is expected.   SD   D   N   A   SA
 16. Physical education equipment and supplies are in sufficient quantity to permit each student to participate fully.   SD   D   N   A   SA
 17. Appropriate facilities are available to accommodate instruction on program goals and objectives.   SD   D   N   A   SA
 18. There is a positive working relationship among superintendent(s), principals, curriculum coordinators, department chairmen, teachers, and students.   SD   D   N   A   SA

Student Characteristics

 1. Students believe they can attain the curriculum objectives.   SD   D   N   A   SA
 2. Students know what they are trying to learn.   SD   D   N   A   SA
 3. Students recognize that the responsibility for learning rests with them.   SD   D   N   A   SA
 4. Students are characterized by an enthusiasm about learning.   SD   D   N   A   SA
 5. Attendance is high.   SD   D   N   A   SA

Appendix C   C - 11

6. Students expect to be successful.   SD   D   N   A   SA

Teacher Characteristics

1. Teachers believe all students can learn and   SD   D   N   A   SA
   expect them to achieve the stated objectives.
2. Teachers are characterized by an enthusiasm   SD   D   N   A   SA
   toward teaching.
3. Teachers are good models of the objectives they   SD   D   N   A   SA
   seek to teach their students.
4. Teachers expect to be successful.   SD   D   N   A   SA
5. Teachers typically spend eight hours daily on   SD   D   N   A   SA
   planning, developing, implementing and/or
   evaluating the program.
6. The staff establishes and maintains positive   SD   D   N   A   SA
   relationships with students.
7. The staff is knowledgeable about the activity   SD   D   N   A   SA
   related structure and function of the body.
8. The staff is competent in the observation and   SD   D   N   A   SA
   assessment of skilled performance.
9. The staff willingly participates in curriculum   SD   D   N   A   SA
   and instructional improvement.
10. The staff plans effectively for daily instruction.   SD   D   N   A   SA
11. The staff maintains an environment in which   SD   D   N   A   SA
    students are consistently challenged to
    achieve stated objectives.

Public Relations

1. There is good communication between teachers   SD   D   N   A   SA
   and school administrators.
2. The department has surveyed the public's know-   SD   D   N   A   SA
   ledge and beliefs about the physical education
   program.
3. The physical education program is held in high   SD   D   N   A   SA
   esteem by the students, community,
   administration and faculty.
4. The K-12 faculty knows what is happening in   SD   D   N   A   SA
   the physical education department.
5. The physical education staff is involved with   SD   D   N   A   SA
   and supports other areas of the school system.
6. The staff makes a consistent effort to interpret   SD   D   N   A   SA
   the program to the public.

Safety and Medical Requirements

1. An appropriate procedure is in place   SD   D   N   A   SA
   and is consistently used for recording and
   filing accident reports.
2. First aid supplies are readily available to all staff SD   D   N   A   SA
   members.
3. The entire staff is qualified to administer first aid. SD   D   N   A   SA

4. A medical record for each student is on file at the school before a student is permitted to participate in physical education.   SD   D   N   A   SA

5. Participation in physical education subsequent to absence due to illness or injury is preceded by medical clearance.   SD   D   N   A   SA

6. Appropriate first aid and/or emergency care are defined and used to guide and care for all injuries.   SD   D   N   A   SA

7. Guidelines for prevention of injuries (including reinjury) are described and practiced by the entire staff.   SD   D   N   A   SA

PROFILE OF PROGRAM STATUS WITH RECOMMENDATIONS

Status Category	Rating Weak ⇔ Strong	Improvement Minimal ⇔ Extensive	Priority	Timeline
Program goals and objectives	1 2 3 4 5	1 2 3		
Curriculum organization	1 2 3 4 5	1 2 3		
Implementation of instruction	1 2 3 4 5	1 2 3		
Student evaluation	1 2 3 4 5	1 2 3		
Program evaluation	1 2 3 4 5	1 2 3		
Qualified personnel	1 2 3 4 5	1 2 3		
K-12 leadership	1 2 3 4 5	1 2 3		
Building leadership	1 2 3 4 5	1 2 3		
Teacher evaluation	1 2 3 4 5	1 2 3		
Professional development	1 2 3 4 5	1 2 3		

NOTES:

Profile of Program Status with Recommendations, page 1

PROFILE OF PROGRAM STATUS WITH RECOMMENDATIONS

Status Category	Rating Weak ◄──► Strong	Improvement Minimal ◄──► Extensive	Priority	Timeline
School climate	1 2 3 4 5	1 2 3		
Student characteristics	1 2 3 4 5	1 2 3		
Teacher characteristics	1 2 3 4 5	1 2 3		
Public relations	1 2 3 4 5	1 2 3		
Safety and medical requirements	1 2 3 4 5	1 2 3		

NOTES:

Profile of Program Status with Recommendations, page 2

References

National Association of Elementary School Principals (1984). *Standards for quality elementary schools: Kindergarten through eighth grade.* Reston, VA: Author.

Vogel, P. G. (1979, Fall). Systematic program design: Evaluation. *Wyoming Journal of Health, Physical Education and Recreation.*

Appendix D

Contributions of Physical Activity to Well-Being[1]

PARTICIPATION IN APPROPRIATE KINDS AND AMOUNTS OF ACTIVITY

1. Promotes changes in brain structure and function in infants and young children. Sensory stimulation through physical activity is essential for the optimal growth and development of the young nervous system.

2. Promotes early cognitive function through imitation, symbolic play, the development of language, and the use of symbols.

3. Assists in the development and refinement of perceptual abilities involving vision, balance, and tactile sensations.

4. Enhances the function of the central nervous system through the promotion of a healthier neuronal network.

5. Aids the development of cognition through opportunities to develop learning strategies, decision making, acquiring, retrieving, integrating information, and solving problems.

6. Fortifies the mineralization of the skeleton and promotes the maintenance of lean body tissue, while simultaneously reducing the deposition of fat.

7. Leads to proficiency in the neuromuscular skills that are the basis for successful participation in games, dances, sports, and leisure activities.

8. Is an important regulator of obesity because it increases energy expenditure, suppresses appetite, increases metabolic rate, and increases lean body mass.

9. Improves aerobic fitness, muscle endurance, muscle power, and muscle strength.

---

[1] *An elaboration of these benefits is found in the 161 statements contained in: Seefeldt, V. D. and Vogel, P. G. (1986). The Value of Physical Activity, Reston, VA: American Alliance for Health, Physical Education, Recreation and Dance. More specific information on the benefits and their sources of support are included in: Seefeldt, V. D. (Ed.), (1986). Physical Activity and Well-Being, Reston, VA: American Alliance for Health, Physical Education, Recreation and Dance.*

10. Is an effective deterrent to coronary heart disease due to its effects on blood lipids, blood pressure, obesity, and capacity for physical work.

11. Improves cardiac function as indicated by an increased stroke volume, cardiac output, blood volume, and total hemoglobin.

12. Is associated with a reduction in atherosclerotic diseases.

13. Promotes a more positive attitude toward physical activity and leads to a more active lifestyle during unscheduled leisure time.

14. Enhances self-concept and self-esteem as indicated by increased confidence, assertiveness, emotional stability, independence, and self-control.

15. Is a major force in the socializing of individuals during late childhood and adolescence.

16. Is instrumental in the development and growth of moral reasoning, problem solving, creativity, and social competence.

17. Is an effective deterrent to mental illness and alleviates mental stress.

18. Improves the psychosocial and physiological functions of mentally and physically handicapped individuals.

19. Deters the depletion of bone mineral and lean body tissue in elderly individuals.

20. Prevents the onset of some diseases and postpones the debilitating effects of old age.

Appendix E

Reported Outcomes Obtained Through Participation In Physical Education Programs[1]

OUTCOME AREA	EVIDENCE
1. ACADEMIC ACHIEVEMENT	INDIRECT
2. ACTIVITY LEVEL	CONVINCING
3. AEROBIC FITNESS	CONVINCING
4. AEROBIC/ANAEROBIC FITNESS	LITTLE
5. AGILITY-COORDINATION	LIMITED
6. ANAEROBIC FITNESS	LITTLE OR NO
7. ATTITUDE	EVIDENCE
8. BALANCE	EVIDENCE
9. BODY COMPOSITION	EVIDENCE
10. BODY SIZE AND SHAPE	LITTLE OR NO
11. DIET	LITTLE OR NO
12. FLEXIBILITY	EVIDENCE (+HIP, -ANKLE)
13. KNOWLEDGE	CONVINCING
14. MATURATION	NO EVIDENCE
15. MOTOR PERFORMANCE	CONVINCING
16. MUSCULAR ENDURANCE	CONVINCING
17. MUSCULAR POWER	CONVINCING
18. MUSCULAR STRENGTH	CONVINCING
19. PERCEPTUAL MOTOR SKILL	EVIDENCE
20. PERSONAL-SOCIAL	LITTLE OR NO
21. PHYSICAL FITNESS	CONVINCING
22. SPEED	EVIDENCE
23. OTHER[2]	EVIDENCE

1 *Summarized from Vogel, P. G. (1986). Chapter 18, p. 455-509. Effects of Physical Education Programs on Children. In V. D. Seefeldt (ed.), Physical Activity and Well-Being. Reston, VA: American Alliance for Health, Physical Education and Dance.*

2 *Cardiovascular risk factors.*

Appendix F

Rating the Importance of Potential Contributions of Physical Activity and Physical Education to Well-Being

The contributions stated below do not automatically occur by participating in various physical activities. Rather, specific kinds of activities, in appropriate intensities, durations, and frequencies must be experienced in order to attain the stated benefits and to avoid potentially detrimental effects.

The statements are directly related to the documented statements included in "Physical Activity and Well-Being."1 Because the list of "potential contributions" exceeds the achievements that are possible within the constraints of instructional time and program resources, the physical education program must attempt to focus on those contributions that have been assigned the highest priority by members of the community. Please help us establish these priorities by rating the importance of each of the following statements. Do not hesitate to ask for clarification of meaning and/or for examples of how the implied content might be included in the curriculum. Rate each statement in accordance with the following scale:

1=not very important (should not be included in a physical education program)
2=limited importance   3=important   4=very important   5=highest importance

Please enter, in the appropriate column, the number that represents what you believe is the appropriate level of importance for each statement.

Potential Contributions	Initial Rating	Final Rating
1. Develop movement proficiency in the fundamental motor skills that underly competence in the physical activities of the culture.	_____	_____
2. Promote the reduction of activity-related injuries.	_____	_____
3. Promote the development and refinement of the perceptual abilities of vision, balance, and tactile sensation.	_____	_____
4. Develop appropriate levels of knowledge regard ing the effects of activity and inactivity on healthy lifestyles and skilled performance.	_____	_____

---

1 Seefeldt, V. D. (1986). *Physical Activity and Well-Being*. Reston, VA: American Alliance for Health, Physical Education, Recreation and Dance.

| Potential Contributions | Initial Rating | Final Rating |

5. Develop an understanding of how to promote the regulation and maintenance of lean body tissue while reducing the deposition of fat. _____ _____

6. Promote the improvement of self-esteem. _____ _____

7. Promote optimal growth and development of certain structural and functional characteristics of the nervous system of infants and young children. _____ _____

8. Contribute to the reduction of activity related health risks. _____ _____

9. Influence desirable shifts in physical activity levels from sedentary to more active. _____ _____

10. Positively influence attitudes toward physical activity. _____ _____

11. Provide knowledge of how to use activity to reduce the incidence of hypokinetic diseases and to postpone the debilitating effects of old age. _____ _____

12. Develop competence in selected leisure activities that can contribute to healthy lifestyles. _____ _____

13. Provide knowledge of how to develop and maintain appropriate levels of physical fitness and motor skill. _____ _____

14. Promote (probably indirectly) academic performance. _____ _____

15. Develop levels of muscular strength, power, endurance, and flexibility that are appropriate for health, protection from injury, and skilled performance. _____ _____

16. Contribute to the development of activity-related personal-social skills. _____ _____

17. Stimulate the growth and development of bone (mineralization, density, width) thus producing a sturdier skeleton. _____ _____

18. Provide the knowledge, skill, and fitness levels necessary to use physical activities to improve emotional stability, reduce anxiety and tension, and increase the ability to cope with stress. _____ _____

19. Develop and maintain appropriate levels of body fat. _____ _____

20. Improve the cardio-respiratory efficiency, capillarization, stroke volume, cardiac output, and lipid profiles and increase total blood volume, maximum work capacity, as well as the ability to sustain high submaximal exercise levels. _____ _____

Appendix G

Examples of Goals and Program Objectives for Physical Education

GOAL 1. To demonstrate competence in selected fundamental motor skills.

Program Objectives

Locomotor

1. walk
2. run
3. leap
4. vertical jump
5. horizontal jump
6. hop
7. skip
8. gallop
9. slide

Object Control

10. underhand roll
11. underhand throw
12. overhand throw
13. dribble (hands)
14. dribble (feet)
15. kick
16. punt
17. catch
18. underhand strike
19. overhand strike
20. forehand strike
21. backhand strike
22. batting

Rationale

1. Fundamental motor skills are prerequisites to successful participation in other games, sports, dances, and activities offered in physical education classes; intramural, athletic and community recreation programs; and other leisure environments.

2. Competence in fundamental motor skills provide the skill base for learning and participation in leisure activities that cannot be taught within the program.

3. Although maturation provides children with the capability or readiness to learn, they must have the opportunity to learn, practice, and refine their skills. While some progress may be made on a trial-and-error basis, instruction increases the efficiency of the learning process.

4. Fundamental motor skills form the movement foundations of many everyday work tasks and play skills of children.

5. Motor skills provide avenues of expression and communication. Learning what the body can do enhances the child's ability to use movement for this purpose.
6. Fundamental motor skills form the basis for activities used to achieve and maintain fitness.
7. Motor behavior in children may be related to academic performance, and cognitive and social development, especially during childhood.
8. Acquisition of proper technique in fundamental motor skills positively influences a person's attitude toward physical activity.

Selection Criteria

1. Include those skills which the community feels are most appropriate for a K-12 physical education program.
2. Include skills that provide the base for other more complex skills within the program.
3. Include skills that provide the base for other more complex skills which are important but not offered in the program.

GOAL 2. To demonstrate knowledge of selected cognitive concepts.

Program Objectives

Beneficial Effects of Activity

1. fitness
2. growth and development
3. weight control
4. stress management
5. aging
6. general health
7. improving physical performance

Detrimental Effects of Activity

8. contraindicated exercises
9. overuse injuries
10. high risk activities

Assessment of Status Related to Selected Health and Performance Factors

11. body composition
12. physical fitness
13. motor performance
14. body mechanics

Appendix G

How to Systematically Alter and Maintain Physical Fitness

15. power development and maintenance
16. strength development and maintenance
17. endurance development and maintenance
18. flexibility development and maintenance
19. posture development and maintenance
20. principles of training
21. aerobic/anaerobic capacity
22. weight control (exercise and nutrition)

How to Systematically Alter Skilled Performance

22. principles of motor learning I
23. principles of motor learning II

Other Factors Which Modify Performance

24. age and maturation
25. gender
26. environmental conditions
27. drugs
28. psychological skills

Injuries

29. injury prevention
30. how to care for common athletic injuries
31. how to rehabilitate common athletic injuries

Movement Terminology - Personal

32. body actions
33. body parts
34. body planes

Movement Terminology - Environmental

35. general space
36. personal space
37. directions in space
38. positions in space

Rationale

1. Benefits of activity are short term. Knowledge of the beneficial and detrimental effects of activity facilitates students' participation in activities outside the school setting.

2. Mere participation in activity does not result in the wide range of benefits possible. Beneficial effects of activity are specific to the kind, amount, duration, frequency, and intensity of the training.

3. No physical education program can provide all activities - thus one should know something about how to learn and maintain a skill.

4. Performance improvement is guided by knowing principles of training.

Selection Criteria

1. Select those concepts that facilitate learning and participation in activity, now and throughout one's lifetime.
2. Select those concepts that clarify the relationship between exercise, health, and performance which have been given priority by the community.
3. Select concepts that relate to other goal areas.
4. Select concepts that are unique to the area of physical education.
5. Select concepts that reinforce the content of other areas of the school curriculum.

GOAL 3. To demonstrate competence on selected indicators of physical fitness.

Program Objectives

Energy Production

1. aerobic
2. aerobic/anaerobic
3. anaerobic

Flexibility

4. neck
5. shoulder
6. hip/spine
7. ankle

Body Composition

8. fat/lean body tissue

Muscular Systems (strength, endurance, power)

9. upperarm
10. forearm
11. shoulder
12. neck
13. abdominal
14. lower back
15. thigh
16. lower leg

Rationale

1. Physical fitness capabilities are necessary to meet a person's biological needs for activity.
2. Physiological adaptations to stressors promote the ability to adapt to stress.
3. Physical fitness capabilities are necessary to provide sufficient strength, endurance, and flexibility necessary to meet the demands of daily living and have a residual for extra needs.
4. Fitness capabilities provide the base (necessary prerequisites) for the efficient acquisition of some skills.
5. The maintenance of proper levels of physical fitness is thought to delay the aging process.
6. Physical fitness capabilities contribute to a positive self-concept.

Appendix G							G-5

7. The maintenance of proper levels of physical fitness contributes to the reduction of certain cardiovascular risk factors and other activity-related health risks.
8. The maintenance of proper percentages of body fat contributes to the prevention of certain degenerative diseases and aids in the maintenance of general health.
9. Physical fitness capabilities contribute to the reduction of injury.
10. The maintenance of proper levels of fitness facilitates normal growth and development.

Selection Criteria

1. Select those indicators which relate most closely to general health attributes.
2. Select indicators which provide a balance of fitness capabilities.
3. Select those indicators which relate most closely to achievement of other stated objectives.
4. Include indicators that may be developed and maintained without excessive equipment.
5. Consider the costs (facilities and equipment) associated with specific indicators of fitness.

GOAL 4. To demonstrate competence in selected body control skills.

Program Objectives

Posture

1. standing posture
2. sitting posture
3. lifting and lowering
4. pushing
5. pulling
6. holding and carrying

Rhythms

7. even beat
8. uneven beat
9. accent

Body Control Skills

10. front vault
11. flank vault
12. foward shoulder roll
13. backward shoulder roll
14. jump and twist
15. front scale
16. beam walk
17. dynamic balance obstacle course
18. rope climb
19. landing

Rationale

1. Skills in body control promote functional body structure (posture-alignment) which positively affects body function.
2. Control of the body in assorted postures and movements promotes a kinesthetic awareness.
3. Selected body control activities provide a deterrent to injury from mishaps such as falling.

4. Body control skills form the foundations of many everyday work tasks and play skills of children.
5. Body control skills provide avenues of expression and communication. Learning body control skills enhances the child's ability to use movement for this purpose.
6. Acquisition of proper technique in body control skills positively influences a person's attitude toward physical activity.
7. Body control skills are prerequisites to successful participation in many games, sports, and activities offered in physical education classes; intramural, athletic, and community recreation programs; and many other leisure environments.
8. Competence in body control skills provides the skill base for learning and participation in leisure activities that may not be available within the local program.
9. Proper posture in various positions and movements helps prevent injury and contributes to general health.

Selection Criteria

1. Include skills which are most applicable to common play activities, work tasks, and everyday experiences.
2. Select skills based on the degree to which they are enabling to other physical education objectives.
3. Select skills that contribute to safe and healthy behaviors.

GOAL 5. To demonstrate performance ability and competence in selected sports, games, and activities.

Program Objectives

The way in which the following games, sports, and activities are categorized is highly subjective and is not meant to be a definitive organizational scheme. Instead, it offers one way of evaluating these sports and games which may be useful in selecting them for inclusion or exclusion in the school curriculum. Each sport selected will contain many program objectives as the term is used in this document. For example, in softball, baserunning, batting, fielding and position play are program objectives unique to softball that would dramatically extend this list. Inclusion of the program objectives for all of the listed activities is beyond the scope of this document.

Also, the category "outdoor" does not mean sports which are played outside, such as football and soccer. In this case it refers to those sports and activities such as hiking and fishing which are often referred to as "outdoor education activities."

	Individual	Dual	Team	Dance	Outdoor	Seasonal
1. aerial darts	X			X		
2. aerobics	X			X		
3. archery	X					
4. backpacking	X				X	
5. badminton		X				
6. basketball			X			
7. bocce ball	X				X	
8. bowling	X					
9. camping	X				X	
10. canoeing	X				X	X
11. climbing	X				X	
12. conditioning	X					
13. croquet		X				X
14. cycling	X					X
15. dance: aerobic	X			X		
16. dance: ballet	X			X		
17. dance: creative	X			X		
18. dance: folk	X	X		X		
19. dance: social		X		X		
20. dance: square		X		X		
21. diving	X				X	
22. fishing	X				X	
23. football			X			X
24. frisbee: skills and games		X	X	X		
25. frisbee: ultimate			X			X
26. golf	X				X	
27. gymnastics: apparatus	X					
28. gymnastics: tumbling	X					
29. handball		X				
30. hiking	X				X	
31. hockey: field			X			X
32. hockey: floor			X			
33. hockey: ice			X			
34. horseshoes		X				X
35. jogging	X					
36. judo			X			
37. karate	X	X				
38. kayaking	X				X	
39. kickball			X			
40. life saving	X					
41. miniature golf		X				
42. newcomb			X			
43. orienteering		X				X
44. paddleball		X				
45. parachute play			X			
46. racquetball		X				
47. riding (horseback)	X				X	
48. riflery	X				X	
49. rock climbing		X				X
50. scuba	X				X	
51. self defense	X					
52. shuffleboard		X				

Selection Criteria

1. Select those traits which occur within the context of physical education activities.
2. Select those traits which are desirable for children to exhibit within a social situation.
3. Select those traits which are important for a child's general personal growth and behavior.
4. Select those traits which facilitate the quality of participation.

Appendix H

Selection, Placement, and Estimation of Needed Instructional Time for Program Objectives

Program Objectives	Priority	Curriculum Level
		K 1 2 3 4 5 6 7 8 9 10 11 12

GOAL 1. To demonstrate competence in selected fundamental motor skills.

Locomotor

1. walk
2. run
3. leap
4. vertical jump
5. horizontal jump
6. hop
7. skip
8. gallop
9. slide

Object Control

10. underhand roll
11. underhand throw
12. overhand throw
13. dribble(hands)
14. dribble(feet)
15. kick
16. punt
17. catch
18. underhand strike
19. overhand strike
20. forehand strike
21. backhand strike
22. batting

Program Objectives	Priority	Curriculum Level
		K 1 2 3 4 5 6 7 8 9 10 11 12

Muscular Systems (strength, endurance, power)

9. upper arm
10. forearm
11. shoulder
12. neck
13. abdominal
14. lower back
15. thigh
16. lower leg

GOAL 4. To demonstrate competence in selected body control skills.

Posture

1. standing posture
2. sitting posture
3. lifting and lowering
4. pushing
5. pulling
6. holding and carrying

Rhythms

7. evenbeat
8. unevenbeat
9. accent

Body Control Skills

10. front vault
11. flank vault
12. foward shoulder roll
13. backward shoulder roll
14. jump and twist
15. front scale
16. beam walk
17. dynamic balance obstacle course
18. rope climb
19. landing

Appendix H

		Curriculum Level				
Program Objectives	**Priority**	K 1 2	3 4 5	6 7 8	9 10	11 12

GOAL 5. To demonstrate performance ability and competence in selected sports, games, and activities

1. aerial darts
2. aerobics
3. archery
4. backpacking
5. badminton
6. basketball
7. bocce ball
8. bowling
9. camping
10. canoeing
11. climbing
12. conditioning
13. croquet
14. cycling
15. dance: aerobic
16. dance: ballet
17. dance: creative
18. dance: folk
19. dance: social
20. dance: square
21. diving
22. fishing
23. football
24. frisbee: skills and games
25. frisbee: ultimate
26. golf
27. gymnastics: apparatus
28. gymnastics: tumbling
29. handball
30. hiking
31. hockey: field
32. hockey: floor
33. hockey: ice
34. horseshoes

Appendix I

Example Instructional Materials and Forms

> **This appendix includes:**
>
> A. Examples of instructional resource materials (assessing activity, teaching-learning activity, drill and game)
>
> B. Blank forms (suitable for reproduction) that can be used to record materials that can be accumulated to

TIME	DIAGRAM AND INSTRUCTIONAL ACTIVITIES	KEY POINTS	EQUIPMENT
	C) those who step with the foot opposite the throwing arm during the windup but who do not bring the ball down and back during this phase	Watch for opposition of movement and restricted arm action	
	D) those who step with the foot opposite the throwing arm, bring the arm down and back but could use some reinforcement in their range of motion and coordination.	Watch for a good pattern but restricted range of motion	
	Level 2 those who throw with all elements of a mature pattern as outlined in instructional objective one		
	Level 3 those who throw with all elements of a mature pattern and also hit a small target		

NOTES, VARIATIONS, HELPFUL COMMENTS (continued from prior page) groups (i.e., 2 and 3). The remainder of the class is then recorded to be in the largest performance group (i.e., 1).

Appendix I I-5

TEACHING-LEARNING ACTIVITY

Program Objective: Overhand throw

Submitted by: Olsen, P.   **Date:** 12-19-87

Grade Level (circle): (K) 1 2 3 4 5 6 7 8 9 10-12

Facilities/Equipment: At least two bean bags for each student, large gym with targets (6' × 6') on 4 walls, restraining line around gym 10-20' from walls

TIME	DIAGRAM AND INSTRUCTIONAL ACTIVITIES	KEY POINTS	EQUIPMENT
10 min	**Setting:** Teacher places students into groups 1, 2, 3, 4, or 5 depending on their level of throwing ability, then moves from station to station giving encouragement, demonstrating, making assessments, and providing feedback. Children throw and when all have thrown, they retrieve their bean bags, return to the restraining line and throw again.	Directions to students	At least 2 bean bags for each student. 5 large (6' × 6') targets.
	Station 1: Children who throw with an anterior-posterior arm pattern, without trunk rotation, are encouraged to turn the non-throwing side to the target and then step toward the target as they throw.	Turn your (left-right-other) side toward the target. Now step to the target as you throw	
	Station 2: Children who step with an ipsilateral pattern are asked to stand with both feet behind the restraining line and then to step over the line with the foot opposite the side of the throwing hand	What foot will step forward? Place your hand on the leg that will step forward. Now step as you turn.	

continued

DRILL NAME: Concentration

Submitted by: Olsen, P.

Date: 2-19-87

Program Objective(s): overhand throw

Grade Level (circle): K 1 2 ③ 4 5 6 7 8 9   Number of Participants (range): 4-5 per group

TIME (Range)	DIAGRAM AND INSTRUCTIONAL ACTIVITIES	KEY POINTS	EQUIPMENT
10 minutes	Children are divided into groups by throwing ability. Each group is to concentrate on the critical element of the overhand throw that must be learned or stabilized for them to become more proficient. Concentration at each of the following stations is on: **Station 1.** Rotating the trunk and stepping as the bean bag is thrown. **Station 2.** Stepping forward with the contralateral foot backward prior to the throw. **Station 3.** Bringing the throwing arm down and backward prior to the throw. **Station 4.** Pivoting on the foot throwing on the same side as the throwing arm during the wind-up phase. More than one group of 4-5 students can be involved at each station.	Children must know on what critical element of the pattern they are to concentrate if the drill is to be effective in skill development	At least 2 bean bags per child

SOURCE:

Appendix I

GAME NAME: What's your score?   **Submitted by:** Olsen, P.   **Date:** 12-19-87

Program Objective(s): overarm throw

Grade Level (circle): (K 1 2 3) 4 5 6 7 8 9 10-12   **Number of Participants (range):** 5 per group

Facilities/Equipment: Sufficient bean bags so that five groups of five children may play at the same time (20 bean bags).

Rules of Play (Object of the Game, Rules, Fouls, Penalties, Scoring): This game builds on the previous drill (concentration) by granting points to those who use the forms that are appropriate for their ability levels and who subsequently strike the targets with the bean bags.

Rules

Each child has a turn in which he/she throws 4 bean bags at a 6' x 6' target, using the overarm pattern. One point is awarded for performing the specific pattern correctly and another for hitting the target. Thus a child could earn 8 points during his/her turn.

Objectives

To have the children learn the part of the skill upon which they must concentrate at their present level of development i.e., at station 1 it is to rotate the body and step with the contralateral foot; at station 2 it is to step with the contralateral foot and bring the hand down and back during the wind-up; at station 3 it is to rotate the trunk and bring the hand with the beanbag down and back when winding up; and at station 4 the objective is to pivot on the foot that is on the side of the throwing hand during the wind-up.

To be effective, children must know how to assess their own and each others' patterns. They will be able to determine whether or not they have hit the target.

SOURCE:

| TIME | DIAGRAM AND INSTRUCTIONAL ACTIVITIES | KEY POINTS | EQUIPMENT |

NOTES, VARIATIONS, HELPFUL COMMENTS

TEACHING-LEARNING ACTIVITY

Submitted by: _____ Date: _____

Program Objective: _____

Facilities/Equipment: _____

Grade Level (circle): K 1 2 3 4 5 6 7 8 9 10-12

TIME	DIAGRAM AND INSTRUCTIONAL ACTIVITIES	KEY POINTS	EQUIPMENT

continued

NOTES / VARIATIONS / HELPFUL COMMENTS:

Appendix I

I - 17

GAME NAME: _____ **Submitted by:** _____ **Date:** _____

Program Objective(s): _____

Grade Level (circle): K 1 2 3 4 5 6 7 8 9 10-12   Number of Players (Range): _____

Facilities/Equipment _____

Rules of Play (Object of the Game, Rules, Fouls, Penalities, Scoring): _____

_____
_____
_____
_____
_____
_____
_____
_____
_____
_____
_____
_____
_____
_____
_____
_____
_____

SOURCE: _____

/372.86V879P>C1/

DATE DUE

FEB 2 5 2003

Demco, Inc. 38-293